RENEWING THE CHURCH BY THE SPIRIT

THEOLOGICAL EDUCATION BETWEEN THE TIMES

Ted A. Smith, series editor

Theological Education between the Times gathers diverse groups of people for critical, theological conversations about the meanings and purposes of theological education in a time of deep change. The project is funded by the Lilly Endowment Inc.

Willie James Jennings
After Whiteness: An Education in Belonging

Chloe T. Sun
Attempt Great Things for God: Theological Education in Diaspora

Amos Yong
Renewing the Church by the Spirit: Theological Education after Pentecost

RENEWING THE CHURCH BY THE SPIRIT

Theological Education after Pentecost

Amos Yong

WILLIAM B. EERDMANS PUBLISHING COMPANY

GRAND RAPIDS, MICHIGAN

Wm. B. Eerdmans Publishing Co.
4035 Park East Court SE, Grand Rapids, Michigan 49546
www.eerdmans.com

26 25 24 23 22 21 20   1 2 3 4 5 6 7

ISBN 978-0-8028-7840-3

Library of Congress Cataloging-in-Publication Data

Names: Yong, Amos, author.
Title: Renewing the church by the Spirit : theological education after
    Pentecost / Amos Yong.
Description: Grand Rapids, Michigan : William B. Eerdmans Publish-
    ing Company, 2020. | Series: Theological education between the
    times | Includes bibliographical references. | Summary: "An argu-
    ment for theological education that is Pentecostal in nature and
    conscious of its place in the twenty-first-century global church"—
    Provided by publisher.
Identifiers: LCCN 2020021728 | ISBN 9780802878403
Subjects: LCSH: Theology—Study and teaching. | Pentecostalism.
Classification: LCC BV4020 .Y66 2020 | DDC 230.071/1—dc23
LC record available at https://lccn.loc.gov/2020021728

This volume is dedicated to Estrelda Y. Alexander and the memory of Vinson H. Synan (1934–2020).

Contents

CONTENTS

CONTENTS

Preface

As a theologian of the Spirit—or pneumatologian—who has been working as a theological educator for almost twenty years (first teaching theology to undergraduates and then, until the time of the writing of the first draft of this manuscript, overseeing doctoral education, initially in a divinity school within a university context and more recently in a tri-school seminary environment), I have in some respects been thinking about this book for two decades. Having written over the years about a range of theological topics from a pneumatological perspective, I now turn to consider theological education. The following pages invite your reflection on how the outpouring of the Spirit at Pentecost two thousand years ago may yet hold some of the keys for engaging many of the challenges that theological education confronts here at the start of the third millennium. Rather than proposing a more concrete program to be enacted, I suggest a pneumatological reimagining of the task of theological education. Readers wondering in parts 1 and 2 of the book about *how* to do theological education more concretely will be rewarded (I hope) in the third part, but those who skip to this last segment will miss out on the *who* and the *why* of theological education elaborated in the first two parts.

My constructive proposals might be considered radical in some quarters, but they are probably more traditionalist when seen from the perspective of my efforts to reappropriate a scriptural imagination. The intention is not to displace completely the present theological education paradigm, but to think more deeply and especially theologically about what we are doing. This kind of reflection inaugurates a process that potentially generates changes more sweeping than currently foreseeable. Such is always the risk of following after the winds of the unpredictable Spirit.

I have written this book not only for theological educators and faculty colleagues but more especially for administrators and church leaders who are wondering how theological education ought to proceed in the present global milieu—here in North America but also around the world—and why or toward what ends. Even more particularly, as a minister credentialed with the American Assemblies of God since 1987 (and dually so as of the year this volume goes to press, now also with the International Church of the Foursquare Gospel), I have written this book from a pentecostal location and especially for those working in institutions of theological education affiliated with pentecostal and charismatic churches and movements around the world.[1] I invite my colleagues in these domains, many of whom are just starting up, to think differently about the work of the Spirit, and about how theological education can be deeply pneumaticized, even radically charismatized, beyond the movement's signal manifestations, and to do so from an ecumenical and global perspective. Christian faith has always been not only after Easter but also after Pentecost, and in that sense theological education also ought to be post-Pentecost, at least as presented in the New Testament. For prospective readers who come from mainline Protestant, evangelical, and other (nonpentecostal) churches and traditions, I believe it indisputable that all Christian theological educators work fundamentally as those filled with the Spirit of Jesus and hence have the opportunity, even the obligation, to think not just theologically but also pneumatologically about our work together. Come, Holy Spirit!

Acknowledgments

I am grateful to Ted Smith, director of the Theological Education between the Times (TEBT) initiative, for his leadership and friendship. Rachelle Green helped to facilitate grant-related events and related activities and always did so with thoughtfulness. My TEBT colleagues Elizabeth Conde-Frazier and Maria Liu Wong also were conversation partners for this manuscript, and I owe them a great debt of gratitude for their honesty and encouragement. I recommend that readers interested in my book and appreciative of its basic thrusts also consult their two books in the series, along with those of Chloe Sun and Keri Day, since all five of us engage intentionally and substantively with pentecostal-charismatic themes and the work of the Spirit in theological education. Dan Aleshire read part 1 of the book in one of its early versions and helped save me from many errors. Ulrike Guthrie and Ted Smith also read the whole manuscript; the former was very helpful in enlivening my prose and cutting away the fat while the latter was perspicacious in his observations even as he was encouraging in his probing questions. Uli and Ted would reappear in innumerable footnotes if I were to indicate at each juncture where the manuscript has been improved by their input. Yet they, and everyone else mentioned here, are to be absolved from blame for errors of fact and interpretation that remain.

Ironically, I began my work with the TEBT initiative when I was leaving Regent University School of Divinity, where I served for nine years (2005–2014), with the final two as dean, and I concluded the first draft of the manuscript of this book shortly before I was appointed, in April 2019, dual-dean here at Fuller Seminary: of its School of Theology and its School of Intercultural Studies (which position I began in July 2019). During the five years of my involvement in the TEBT, I served as faculty member in the School of Intercultural Studies and found myself immersed formally and for the first time in the field of missiology. I could not have written this book without the welcome I received from my missiological colleagues and assistance in my initiation into mission studies. In hindsight, what I have written here gestated long before I was inundated in decanal work here at Fuller, although I think in revising the manuscript during the copyediting and proofreading stages that it has been surprisingly prescient for my present work.

Yet the roots of this volume of course precede my time at Fuller Seminary. Over two decades ago, Kelly Monroe published her book *Finding God at Harvard* (Zondervan, 1997). Since then, the Council for Christian Colleges and Universities (CCCU) has emerged and announced a Christ-centered approach to Christian higher education. A few years ago, a Regent colleague, Dale Coulter, and I wondered: If God and Christ are now to be found in higher education, what about the Holy Spirit? This led us to begin working on a book tentatively titled *Finding the Holy Spirit at a Christian University: Renewing Christian Higher Education*, intended first and foremost for those laboring within, associated with, and interested in the work of the CCCU. The volume you hold in your hands can be read as a prequel to that coauthored work, with the argument here focused more specifically on theological education.

My Fuller graduate assistants, Nok Kam and Jeremy Bone, were very helpful in obtaining research materials. Particular thanks are owed to Jeremy for help setting the format for citations.

For almost three decades, my wife, Alma, has been a faithful partner in my journey through theological education. For the TEBT initiative and this book, I had to make over a half-dozen additional half-week trips out of town that she gracefully endured. Her steadfast love has always supported and encouraged my endeavors. I always marvel at the gift of grace that her companionship represents to me.

This book is dedicated to Estrelda Y. Alexander and Vinson H. Synan. Vinson was the dean at Regent University School of Divinity and invited me to join that faculty in the spring of 2005. I stayed at Regent for nine years (still longer than anywhere else in my life to date) and enjoyed my work with him and other Regent colleagues while there. Vinson's own legacy is secure as one of the premier historians of North American Pentecostalism, even as he has long been recognized in the pentecostal world as a leading theological educator and effective and innovative administrator. Yet Alma and I know that he has been able to accomplish as much as he has over the decades only because of the contributions of his wife, Carol! During the winter of 2020, while this book was being copyedited, I was able to share this paragraph with Carol Lee, who read it to Vinson a few weeks before he passed into the Divine presence.

Estrelda was a faculty member at Regent University School of Divinity when I arrived. We connected quickly, organizing two conferences together—one on women in pentecostal-charismatic ministry and the other on black pentecostal-charismatic Christianity—and then coediting the two volumes emanating from those events. Easily the most prolific and foremost theologian of the African American pentecostal tradition, Estrelda is one of the more visionary, courageous, and persevering colleagues I have ever known and been privileged to work with. Her departure to found William Seymour College left a big gap in our divinity school faculty, but we knew that she could not be deterred from this vocational call. Alma and I are grateful to God for the lives, work, and friendship of these leading scholars of the global pentecostal movement.

Unless otherwise noted, all Scripture quotations are from the New Revised Standard Version of the Bible.

Introduction

This introduction lays out in brief the current global sociohistorical context within which anxiety about theological education is being felt, presents the theological thesis and thrust of the book, and outlines its basic orientation and presentation.

Flattening Theological Education: Whence and Whither in the Twenty-First Century?

Theological education exists not in a sociohistorical vacuum but in a political economy that is currently squeezing higher education more generally. As misleading as are journalistic metaphors for those desiring more rigorous thoughtfulness, I still think Thomas Friedman's best-selling book titled *The World Is Flat* helpfully locates our present situation.[1] Friedman's notion of *flatness* and two interrelated motifs—*connectedness* and *networks*—can be used as a springboard to characterize what is presently going on.

By identifying the world as *flat*, Friedman is theorizing about the collaborative, horizontal world created by the forces of globalization. A flat world eliminates both the institutional hierarchy that dominated the medieval and early modern world and the intermediaries that facilitated the transfer of goods, services, and knowledge. Supply and demand occur less and less as chains of agents, organizations, and processes, and more and more as direct exchanges. Further, the global economy is also constituted by transnational linkages: work is outsourced, offshored, and uploaded, directly establishing individuals in the informational economy. This is not to say that every person is now competing against everyone else, since there remains a gap between those able to enter into and reap the benefits of this flattened economy and those not so privileged for various reasons such as poverty, underdeveloped national and social infrastructures, and lack of education.

Connectedness refers first and foremost to the primary medium of such global linkages: the technologically sustained and expanding Internet. The haves and the have-nots are surely devolving into those with and without access to the digital world. If for Friedman the Internet is the conduit primarily of economic globalization, sociologist Manuel Castells suggests that this central pipeline of the third millennium's informational economy also directs the many flows that affect the cultural, social, and political relationships of human lives.[2] Social media is increasingly the platform upon which personal and collective identities are forged, ideologies are developed and challenged, and political campaigns are carried out. Paradoxically, though individual voices are being amplified as never before, the globally connected stage is now a cacophony of sounds.

What characterizes our flat and connected humanity is that it is *networked*. Earlier communal and national links are being replaced by very fluid and dynamic electronic, social, organizational, transnational, and relational connections mediating the sharing, transfer, and mobilization of people, wealth, knowledge, and power. Arguably this informational and networked economy allows more individual autonomy and encourages innovative creativity precisely through the cross-fertilization that results when persons with divergent backgrounds converge on common initiatives and interests.[3] The challenge is that the older social structures are practically superfluous in this new regime. Its leveling out touches every sphere of human life around the globe, except perhaps one: the chasm between rich and poor. Networks come and go, expand and contract, overlap and diverge, or fluctuate and morph as members (individuals or organizations) are drawn in or phase out.

Higher education in general is being radically disrupted amid these trends. Its elitism no longer holds its earlier prestige, and its products are increasingly professional credentials to meet dynamic market demands. Formerly funded by taxpayers and the welfare state, higher education is now increasingly privatized and part of the market economy. Education is thus opening up, not only because of the Internet but also because of our changing informational economy.[4]

Renewing Theological Education: After Pentecost

Theological education cannot avoid the impact of these broader developments. Its institutions used to rely on hierarchical ecclesial connections that are now fraying in a flattened, connected, and networked world. Further, if institutions of theological education formerly served Christian churches, the nature of ecclesiality is itself being called into question in a diversifying post-Christian and postcolonial world, to the point that theological educators are now less sure about the identity of their primary constituents. How might theological education reconstruct itself in a postmodern, post-Western, post-Enlightenment, and even post-Christendom age?

While I don't fault others for resorting to practical responses to the crisis in theological education—whether to secure financial viability, replenish a diminishing student enrollment, or establish relevant programs and curricula for the consumer market—my own approach is decidedly theological. Though others have preceded me down this path,[5] I both propose a broader theological analysis of education and cast a more precise theological vision.

My own ecclesial location, the modern pentecostal movement, rarely talks about an ecclesial crisis and more often dis-

3

penses a triumphalist rhetoric, buoyed by demographers touting how world Christianity is growing largely because of the achievements of these pentecostal and charismatic movements. How can theological education serve these developments at the vanguard of world Christian growth but also be more subdued about the inevitable comings and goings of social forms? The key, I think, is to be both ecclesiological and more fully pneumatological.

Because the church exists as the body of Christ and as the fellowship of the Spirit (2 Cor. 13:13), there is no nonpentecostal church—no people of God upon whom the Spirit has not been poured out (Acts 2:33). I would go further and argue that part of the crisis of the church today has to do with its Pentecost-related pneumatic aspects not being recognized, or at best being marginalized. To ask about the role of the Spirit in theological education, then, ought to be of interest to all who seek to root such efforts more deeply in the redemptive work of God in our time. How might theological education be reconceptualized from this perspective after both Easter *and* Pentecost?

The renewal of theological education in a flat, connected, and networked world can be found by reconsidering the primordial Pentecost outpouring of the Spirit. This pneumatic event not only initiated the embryonic church but also catalyzed the church's mission in and to the world. Thus, every chapter of the present book engages at some level the Lukan narrative and considers the implications of the Pentecost event and its aftermath for contemporary theological education in a third-millennium context that is deeply glocal—both local and global. What I try to retrieve, however, is not just a prescribed number of steps toward sustainability or profitability. Instead, I wish to nurture a kind of theological sensibility—a pneumatological imagination, more precisely—that, when confronted with specific curricular, pedagogical, and policy questions in dynamically shifting environments, can explore effective contextual responses by asking, in effect: *What has the Spirit done? What might the Spirit be doing? What would the Spirit do? What would the Spirit wish for or empower us to do?* In short, mine is a theological re-visioning of theological education that cultivates a hermeneutical and methodological imagination for renewing the church in its participation in the mission of God in the twenty-first century. It is a vision retrieved from the past but intended for the future.

Overview of the Book

The movement of the book's three parts follows this ecclesiological, missiological, and educational arc. It considers education holistically as involving not only minds (the cognitive) but also bodies (the affective) and activities (the behavioral)—heads, hearts, and hands.[6] Such a triadic conceptualization is both amenable to historic theological explication in terms connecting orthodoxy (beliefs) to orthopathy (desires) and orthopraxy (practices), and consistent with the ethos and sensibilities of the relational, affective, and pragmatic spirituality of pentecostal and charismatic churches and movements.[7] Our journey begins with the church as the heart of theological education (the *who*), then proceeds through the church's missional vocation that charts the telos (or purpose) and hands of theological education (the *why*), and arrives at the intellectual core of the enterprise that can be comprehended as the task or "head" of theological education (the *how*).

Part 1 explains the evolution of the church in our increasingly flat—that is, connected and networked—world. We begin by discussing the church and its theological-educational fortunes in North America (our immediate location and context), move to consider how even this space and reality are progressively flattened vis-à-vis the so-called Global South, and then review the internal dynamics of such flattening that are shaping new ecclesial forms and expressions. The discussion in part 1 of the book looks at the primary audiences and constituencies of theological education. How are such theological learners being shaped by flattening forces? And what social and institutional dynamics can be drawn from observable ecclesiological trends that can help us understand better what theological institutions are engaging or ought to serve? My argument in these three chapters is that theological education needs to engage the rapidly de-institutionalizing forms of the twenty-first-century church and yet attend to the search for spiritual experience and significance that marks contemporary religious life.

Even if we manage to correlate theological education better with its consumers (learners in ever-mutating types of churches), the question arises: To what ends? Unless we can be clear about the goals of such churches, the rationale for theological education will teeter. The telos of the church is the coming reign of God proclaimed by Jesus and the apostolic church, and it is this missional trajectory that orients the *why* of the church and therefore ought also to direct the thrust of theological education. Part 2 of the book thus explores the public theological content, economic shape, and personal character of such a missional imagination. I will urge that what the church does in her participation in the *missio Dei* is live out its witness in the public environment, embody its life in the global economic cosmopolis, and shape learners for spirited, networked, and faithful discipleship-citizenship.

These ecclesiological and missiological considerations then set us up for a deeper burrowing into the task of theological education in part 3. Here is where I flesh out in more specificity (while being thoroughly theological and pneumatological) the work of theological education given its audience (the church) and its purpose (the *missio Dei*). Chapters 7 through 9 thus look at the curricular/disciplinary, pedagogical, and scholarly aspects of that undertaking. What does it mean to be intentional about the work of the Spirit in these aspects of the theological educational task? Throughout, I connect what happens within the educational endeavor with the ecclesial and missional discussions. The goal is to re-vision theological education for a spiritually vital and connected-networked global humanity.

Yet the path to that goal of a Spirit-ed theological education is accessible solely through the Spirit of Pentecost. Driving my argument is the work of the Spirit poured out upon all flesh—

especially as recounted by the Third Evangelist in his two books in the Christian canon: Luke and Acts—to form Jesus followers into an ecclesial and missional community of disciples. Can theological education today be bolstered by such an ancient image and narrative? I believe so, and I invite you to an extended consideration of that conviction.

1

CHURCH AMID WORLD CHRISTIANITIES

The Heart and Soul of Theological Education

Theological Education and the (Western) Church

Equipping the Body of Christ

Theological education is surely a cognitive enterprise, and such human cognition is socially embodied. Hence, all learning, theological study included, derives from our kinesthetic embodiment and interpersonal relations, and therefore is more than merely abstracted or generalized concepts. One way to get at this embodied dimension of theological education is to situate its tasks and activities within the heart of such a palpable and interactive reality, the church.

Yet when we pause to ask, *What is the church?*, we realize that its shifting forms demand reflection. The hierarchically organized church of Western Christendom, for instance, is no longer the only or perhaps even the dominant form today. But if theological education as we know it largely served that vertically layered sociality, what happens when that body changes its form, for instance, by spreading out and extending itself horizontally instead? Part 1 of this book explores precisely this question, starting in the North American context (this chapter), especially the United States, expanding toward a more global horizon (chap. 2), and then observing ecclesial and religious trends in glocal contexts (chap. 3). Our goal is to understand *church* in its organic relationality and experiential spirituality so as to imagine emerging and new forms of theological education.

I begin this chapter with a very brief overview of the waxing and waning of distinct groupings of theological education across the last generation, and then explore the aesthetic forms and social/institutional implications of these ecclesial dynamics. Second, I trace the ways this consideration of the *what* and *how* of the church's organic transmission raises the question of the nature of ecclesiality. In the third section I suggest that from these developments comes a more charismatic and experiential understanding of the church as the fellowship of the Spirit. My goal in this chapter is to establish as firm a grounding as possible for theological education in the shifting North American ecclesial milieu in order to consider the wider global landscape.

What Church? "Evangelicalizing" Theological Education

What is the nature of the church that theological educators are supposed to be engaging and serving? We begin with some hard data from the Association of Theological Schools (ATS), the leading accreditation organization for seminaries, theological schools, divinity schools, and other graduate-level purveyors of theological education in North America.[1] From 2000 to 2017, the total head count of students enrolled in ATS-affiliated schools rose slightly, from 72,310 to 73,175. One might think the enterprise of theological education thus remains a healthy one. However, when we consider the numbers from the perspective of the relevant ecclesial movements, we find Roman Catholic enrollment has decreased slightly over the same period (from 8,238 to 7,516), while two other major currents have been starkly divergent. Mainline Protestants have suffered an almost 30 percent loss, from 22,991 to 16,479, while evangelicals[2] have carried the bulk of the growth, increasing 18.5 percent, from 41,508 to 49,190, since 2000.

Similarly, the total number of mainline Protestant institutions of theological education affiliated with ATS has declined from 97 in 2000 to 89 in 2017, and their prognosis for the future is not rosy.[3] On the other hand, evangelical schools have grown by over a third during this same eighteen-year period, from 89 to 120. In 2000, evangelicals constituted 37 percent of all ATS schools and 57.4 percent of the total head count across these same institutions. By 2017, they were in the majority on both fronts: 56.7 percent of the schools and two-thirds, or about 67 percent, of the total number of students.

In one way, this ought not to be surprising, since it has been clear for over a generation that conservative churches have been holding strong if not growing in some quarters and that mainline Protestant denominations have been struggling to maintain their levels, if not actually failing. These trends have persisted, generally speaking (even if with important qualifications). Cumulatively, for instance, membership in denominations like the Disciples of Christ, the American Baptist Convention, the Evangelical Lutheran Church in America, the Episcopal Church, the Presbyterian Church USA, the United Church of Christ, and the United Methodist Church has diminished from over 18 percent of the total USA population to under 14 percent from 2007 to 2014, numbers consistent with the downward trend of over four decades.[4]

On the whole, evangelical churches have resisted such a steep loss of adherents and, in some cases, have continued to expand. From 2007 to 2014, these churches increased from 51 to 55 percent of all Protestants (Pew, 14) and, in raw numbers, from under 60 million to over 62 million adherents (Pew, 9). Consider four clearly evangelical denominations: the Assemblies of God, the Presbyterian Church of America, the Christian and Missionary Alliance, and the Evangelical Free Church of America. From 2000 to 2017, combined approximate membership and adherence in these bodies increased from 2,631,431 to 4,254,169—an increase of over 60 percent.[5] This does not include informal estimates (which is all we have) of the largest pentecostal denomination in North America, the African American Church of God in Christ, whose membership of approximately 2.25 million in 1988 more than doubled to about 5.5 million by 2012. However these numbers are counted, we see a correlation between the increase in evangelical institutions of theological education and their numbers of students, on the one hand, and the growth of evangelical churches on the other.

Now for three major qualifications: First, people affiliated with evangelical and pentecostal churches and denominations in North America ought not to rest smugly as if they are immune to these wider demographic trends. As we shall see, growth in these sectors is largely attributable to immigration from outside of North America. In fact, the next two chapters document what many evangelical and pentecostal ecclesiarchs are keenly aware of: that immigration aside, their "tribes" have not just plateaued but are actually losing members.[6] That is why I am resisting championing contemporary evangelical or pentecostal Christianity as the way forward for theological education in the next generation and am instead identifying how the spirituality of encountering the Divine nurtured in these movements highlights how people are looking for religious vitality first and foremost rather than another form of institutional religiosity.

Second, then, and related to the preceding point: even though mainline churches are dwindling, a so-called confessing church movement has emerged over the last few decades, some wings of which operate within mainline denominations (like the Alliance of Confessing Evangelicals within the Presbyterian Church USA) and others diverge from their mother denominations (like those distinguishing themselves from the Episcopal Church, such as the Anglican Church in North America, the Anglican Mission in the Americas, and the Convocation of Anglicans in North America). These evangelical types constitute 41 percent of Lutherans, 36 percent of Presbyterians, and 15 percent of Congregationalists, for instance (Pew, 23). The future of these bodies may or may not retain the evangelical label, but they at least caution against any dismissal of Protestantism that the decline thesis might assume.[7]

Finally, these confessing movements are often both evangelical and charismatic, and many are shaped by and connecting back to the charismatic renewal that unfolded in mainline Protestant churches from the 1960s to the early 1980s. In fact, more than a third of US adults describe themselves as "born again," and 22 percent of Roman Catholics and 18 percent of Orthodox believers also embrace this label (Pew, 31–32). As such born-again evangelicals are also often charismatic *and* pentecostal in their sensibilities if not commitments, some researchers have begun to talk about the "pentecostalization" of the North American evangelical movement.[8] These developments are both important for discerning implications for theological education, as the rest of this chapter will detail, and consistent with what is happening among these denominations globally, as we shall see in the next chapter. For our purposes, then, while it is true that strictly mainline groups are fading numerically, the labels are slippery and not altogether helpful since they continue to include evangelical (and charismatic) students who are enrolled in both evangelical and mainline schools and are pursuing theological education.[9]

All of the above begs the question: What about the elusive category of *evangelical*? On the one hand, we might easily recognize all churches affiliated with the National Association of Evangelicals as belonging in this fold.[10] On the other hand, David Bebbington, and many others following him, has suggested that *evangelical* be understood adjectivally, as a set of characteristics—for example, biblicism (focused on the Bible), crucicentrism (concentrated on the cross of Christ as essential for the salvation of the world), conversionism (insistent on personal repentance and devotion), and activism (commitment to missionary activity at the grassroots sociopolitical level)—that defines a certain kind of piety.[11] Evangelical commitments in this pietistic sense are deeply experiential, revolving around what is often testified about as a vital and personal encounter and ongoing relationship with Jesus Christ.

Even if theological education in North America is feeling great strain, there are still opportunities for engaging the evangelical movement, broadly speaking. Yet we need to keep in mind the complexities. Some of the institutions the ATS includes under the evangelical label are clearly denominationally affiliated, for example, Covenant Theological Seminary (Presbyterian Church of America), Alliance Theological Seminary and Ambrose Seminary (both Christian and Missionary Alliance), and Trinity Evangelical Divinity School (Evangelical Free Church of America). Others are identified via various categorizations: for example, as pentecostal (at least eight by my count) or as inter/multidenominational (60 percent of the schools on the list) or as nondenominational (half of the list).[12] A few, like the Trinity Episcopal School for Ministry, serve the charismatic Anglican Church in North America and other like-minded groups, and (I assume) are included within the *evangelical* count.[13]

How Church? Networking Theological Education

Even if we accept that there are opportunities for further theological education in the evangelical movement in North America, loosely comprehended, there are other considerations. In one direction, such "evangelicalism" is currently experiencing another identity crisis, this one the realization that many of the majority-white denominations and churches within the movement catapulted Donald J. Trump to the American presidency in 2016 and have since remained among his administration's most ardent supporters. As a result, many have disavowed the evangelical identification, and even those who do not wish to or cannot completely disassociate themselves are qualifying their relationship to the evangelical movement.[14] From this perspective, what is called *evangelicalism* remains a contested and conflicted reality, and it remains to be seen whether and how this population of persons and churches will engage with theological education going forward, especially since the kind of populism rampant in these sectors is often suspicious of the elitism perceived in the educational enterprise.

Yet many within the North American church are evangelical in character without ever using that name or label to identify themselves. The ATS categories of inter/multidenominational and nondenominational actually encapsulate two truths: first, that American Protestantism is fast shifting from a denominationally defined movement, at its height in the mid-twentieth century, to what is effectively a postdenominational era,[15] one character-ized much less by formal (denominationally delineated) ecclesial ties and more by relational dynamics; and second, that American Protestantism as a group is also dissipating. Not surprisingly, the Pew report observes that *nondenominational* segments of the church enjoyed their most significant growth in the years leading up to 2014: almost one in five evangelicals situate themselves in such churches, as do 13 percent of Protestants and 6.2 percent of all adults in the country (Pew, 15, 26), thus highlighting what might be called a nondenominatializing trend within the move-ment.[16] Hence, students who are evangelical at ATS institutions may be so because of their spirituality and practices—including those explicated by Bebbington—even if they do not primarily identify as such. Certainly the 120 ATS-affiliated schools gath-ered under the *evangelical* rubric (as of 2017) are servicing not just members of established evangelical denominations but also those whose piety and practice make them feel at home in such institutions, including students who still belong to mainline Protestant denominations. If this is the case, evangelical insti-tutions may attract students who are less invested in the label than they are looking to nurture certain historic values, commit-ments, and practices, even if recent events across the contempo-rary North American evangelical church at large have called this into question.

There is one more complicating point related to the so-called evangelicalizing trend of North American theological education: the charismatic, neocharismatic, classical pentecostal, and neo-pentecostal undercurrents to these evangelical denominations or individuals. A fundamental realignment is occurring: North American denominational structures are giving way to dynamic networks connected by ministries, charisms, and relationships. Bureaucratic hierarchies are being replaced by charismatic com-plexes, and professionally certified ministers by relationally oriented mentors.[17] It would not be inaccurate to say these are all evangelicals, but many will aver that the living experience of the Holy Spirit's work rather than formal affiliations or any identification with labels defines their life and ministry. What drives these ministries are grassroots and organically multiplying networks of relationships that are now also mediated by the Internet.[18]

It is no wonder that traditional forms of theological education are in trouble. Seminaries and similar institutions that two generations ago catered to and were directly subsidized by denominations now have to be reinvented almost completely if they are to engage with an electronically flickering, socially amorphous, and charismatically churning complex of relationships. Surely evangelicals will be an important feature in the domain of theological education for the foreseeable future, but it may well be even more urgent that theological educators heed not the label of evangelicalism but the experiential and charismatic spirituality that surges through these most vital arteries of a movement that is both Christ centered and Bible based, and also Spirit empowered. Ecclesiality in the current moment is being generated less and less through denominational protocol and more and more by relational and democratized charisma, that is, the charismatic activity of leaders and lay members.[19] We need a network ecclesiology to understand anew what the church is becoming and to recalibrate our systems of theological education in modalities and directions relevant to and able to interface with these dynamic virtual and social realities.[20]

Anticipating Church: Charismatizing Theological Education

The question this part of the book poses is: *What is the nature of the church of the twenty-first century that theological education is serving?* This chapter began by focusing on the North American landscape. So far, it has noted two interrelated points: that the preceding generation has seen the qualified expansion of an evangelical presence in North American theological education that correlates with the diminishing of mainline Protestant denominations; and that this evangelicalizing dynamic has been fed, at least in part, by pentecostal and charismatic undercurrents, consistent with the ethos although not with the institutional forms of the evangelical movement.

What we are seeing aligns with the observation that we are completing the transition from the so-called age of Christendom to whatever is coming after. While not wishing to conjure up all the baggage inherent in this notion, I do mean to use "Christendom" to name the hierarchically operationalized and institutionally mediated outward forms of the historic church. In some respects, the beginning of the end of Christendom was the Protestant Reformation, both in its doctrine of the priesthood of all believers and in its polity of congregationalism that insisted on the autonomy of locally established bodies of believers rather than episcopal or presbyterian systems. Evangelical conversionism can be understood as one major historic expression of the role of believers vis-à-vis the institutional church, even as the postdenominational phenomenon can be seen as a further flattening out of ecclesial authority from confessionally ordered structures to relational networks.

To be clear: the so-called end of Christendom obviously does not mean that denominations have ceased to exist or that institutional forms of the church have completely disappeared. The Roman Catholic Church and its sixty institutions of theological education in North America have held their own. Yet within the Protestant world, at least, we are working less and less with learners who are denominationally formed and more and more with those shaped by a network imagination. These are distinct modalities of formation that invite both different styles of teaching and learning and discrete expressions of the scholarly vocation.[21] The future may well bring unexpected convergences, yet these not-yet-apparent conjunctions will be mediated by the current trends.

If one of the mottos coming out of the Reformation was *ecclesia reformata, semper reformanda*—the church reformed, always requiring further reform—then five centuries later such reforma-

19

tion is being facilitated in many ways by pentecostal and charismatic renewal.[22] This is arguably an extension of the Reformation commitment to the sovereignty of God, since the emphasis of pentecostal and charismatic renewal is on neither the agency of believers nor the agenda of churches, but on the initiating and prior work of the Holy Spirit. Intriguingly, however, the renewing work of the Spirit galvanizes personal agency and sparks ecclesial initiatives, more so from the (historical) ground up than the (institutional) top down. The question is how theological education in the present moment can engage with the continuously reforming and renewing work of the Spirit.

One scriptural text relevant for retrieval is 1 Corinthians 12. This passage provides at least three notions I find helpful for thinking about the nature of the church awaiting what comes after Christendom.

First, the church is not just the body of Christ in all its organicity but also the fellowship of the Spirit in all her charismaticity.[23] It is the encounter with the living Christ by his Spirit and then confession of Jesus as Lord by the same Spirit (1 Cor. 12:3). It involves the experience of the spiritual gifts (12:4-10), given and "activated by one and the same Spirit, who allots to each one individually just as the Spirit chooses" (12:11), that combines to constitute the living body of Christ (12:12-13). Charisma and *ecclesia* are thus co-inaugurative.

Second, precisely because of the Spirit's work, every member of the body has reciprocal gifts to be respected and contributions to be welcomed. In fact, "the members of the body that seem to be weaker are indispensable" (12:22), so that we all (ought to) suffer *and* rejoice together (12:26). Such a charismatic ecclesiality thus honors not just institutional prerogatives but also grassroots initiatives. If every member of the body is endowed with and enabled by the Spirit's gifts, then every voice counts and every agent is to be heard, observed, and discerned for what he or she has to offer the fellowship of the Spirit. Ecclesial authoritarianism and hierarchicalism hereby give way to pietistic interpersonalism and organic interrelationalism.

Third, Saint Paul ends this section by connecting Spirit-gifted individuals with what some might also call offices (apostles, prophets, teachers) and ministerial forms (working of miracles, healing, speaking in tongues or interpreting them [12:28–29]), all in the expectation of forming messianic congregations as communities of love (1 Cor. 13). Collectives of the former open up to forms of social organization that invite corporate commitments beyond individual concerns. Hence, I believe we can shift here to consider also the Spirit's work above the level of individuals: at that of congregations, communities, and networks, and even at higher levels incorporating the shifting structures of Christendom, whether those perceived as more enduring (e.g., the Roman Catholic hierarchy), as waning (mainline Protestant denominational structures), or as emerging (as discussed in the next chapter). We can always ask, at each of these levels, what the animating charism of the Spirit is, so that ecclesial reformation within each domain can be discerned in relationship to the same Spirit's renewing work.[24] In so doing, we open up a teleological dimension to the identity of the church—not just who she is but also what she does (see part 2 below).

If the church, past, present, and future, can be understood as the fellowship of the Spirit, how might theological education not just serve and engage with but also inhabit this pneumatic and charismatic dynamic? Can theological education be imagined as being motivated by the pathos of the Spirit, as being disciplined by the pedagogy of the Spirit, or as nurtured by a spirited life of the mind? What does it mean to think about theological education as charismatic activity, or of theological formation in charismatizing modalities? How can we reconsider the diversity of the church as a pentecostal and ecumenical gift for theological education?[25]

Note here that we are asking ourselves neither personality-type nor sociological questions. In some respects, we cannot get away completely from notions of the charismatic that relate to both larger-than-life leaders and the kinds of movements they galvanize. Of course, there are charismatic leaders in the contemporary network Christianities we have been discussing, even apostles and prophets, as some in their ranks self-identify. Yet the charismatic prophet's work (1 Cor. 14) is always normed by the love of God manifest in Jesus Christ and made available as the fruit of the Spirit (1 Cor. 13). So, while wishing to be cautious about naïve receptions of attractive spiritually empowered leaders, it would also be a mistake to throw out the proverbial baby of charismatic manifestations with the bathwater of ongoing movements of the Spirit in every age, since the gifts of the Spirit are for *all* members of the body, not just a few.

Our question is or ought to be a fundamentally theological one. If the contemporary church is characterized by grassroots and networked movements, how can we as theological educators discern and name the character, arcs, and trajectories of these movements as part of what the Spirit is doing today? And what does this mean for our work? The focus of this chapter has been fairly narrow—North American ecclesial trends related to the ATS. In the next chapter we go beyond this hemisphere.

2

Theological Expansion of the Church Catholic

Engaging the People of God

This chapter expands our discussion culturally, geographically, and ecumenically, considering the worldwide *ekklēsia* or church universal and its exponentially pluriform expressions of the people of God. It introduces little new in the ecclesiological conversation—the church has always been comprehended as one, holy, apostolic, and catholic—but asks about the nature of such catholicity vis-à-vis the task of contemporary theological education. How does our understanding of the church as a universal people of God inform what theological educators (ought to) do?[1]

I begin by asking about the transnational connections emanating from and emerging within the North American ecclesial domain, and then shift my perspective from the North American West to the global "rest" to ask: What does theological education look like from the perspective of the so-called Global South or majority world? How do we discern trajectories of the enterprise of theological education when we foreground the efforts of those in Asia, Africa, and Latin America rather than marginalize them as mere extensions of Western (and North American) efforts? I conclude by complementing the previous chapter's discussion of charismatic theological education with the notion of a "pentecostal" approach to theological education for a global and catholic people of God filled with the Spirit of Jesus.

Our goal in the first part of this book is to grasp more clearly what I am calling the heart and soul of theological education— the church. Our task is to take its current pulse and then to diagnose its vitality in order to prescribe a mode of theological education that attends better to the inner wellsprings of the global church. If we are centered in the work of the triune God, we shall see that the heart of theological education ought to be focused on the whole people of God, all those who seek to live in the way of Jesus as encountered in, experienced through, and led by his Spirit. The global vivacity and catholic shape of this way are the locus of this chapter.

The "Browning" Church: Education across Borders

Although the notion of the "brown church" refers more specifically to the growth of Latino/a populations in the North American ecclesial landscape—trending upward from 13 percent in 2007 to 16 percent in 2014[2]—it is also an apt metaphor for the correlated decline in Caucasians and the increase in all other groups combined.[3] Generally, and at the national level, while the percentage of the population who identify as white declined (from 71 percent in 2007 to 66 percent in 2014), the total of all other groups expanded from 29 to 34 percent over the same period (Pew, 5, 52). No doubt a significant part of this shift has been generated by immigration. Approximately one-fourth of all Christians in the United States are immigrants (meaning either first-generation arrivals from other countries or their children). The Roman Catholic Church in this country has been most deeply affected by immigration, with about four in ten Catholics now coming from elsewhere (Pew, 54). Among Protestants, 16 percent of evangelicals and 23 percent of Pentecostals are immigrants (Pew, 123). These trends are expected to accelerate.

In the preceding chapter I mentioned that the African American Church of God in Christ (COGIC) was the largest pentecostal denomination. But African American evangelicals and pentecostals surge beyond denominational bounds. They are distributed not only across various black historic churches but also across white churches, and increasingly among nondenominational congregations and networks.[4] Unsurprisingly, then, many of these evangelical and pentecostal types are not opting to attend the seven historically black seminaries or theological/divinity schools (with the addition of a Seventh-day Adventist university in Alabama in 2018), and even COGIC's Charles Harrison Mason Seminary, which operates through the Interdenominational Theological Center in Atlanta, is having trouble attracting students. Yet African Americans constitute over 12 percent of ATS enrollment, a rate consistent with their overall demographic in the country, so any discussion of the opportunities facing theological education today must keep in mind their history.[5]

A distinct but complicating factor in these considerations is migrant African churches that have been coming to North America over the last few decades.[6] The Ghanaian Church of Pentecost, for instance, has a mission-driven, evangelistic, church-planting strategy that (as of late 2018) has produced approximately 220 churches across the continent—up from 152 congregations at the end of 2014[7]—and led to the establishment of a school: Pentecost Bible College in Wayne, New Jersey.[8] Similarly, as of the end of 2018, the Nigerian Redeemed Christian Church of God (RCCG), another African pentecostal church, has about 950 congregations across the United States and three levels of schools for ministerial and lay training: the Redeemed Christian Bible College and Seminary in Dallas, Texas, currently accredited with TRACS (Transnational Association of Christian Colleges and Schools); the Redeemer's Leadership Institute; and the RCCGNA (Redeemed Christian Church of God North America) School of Disciples.[9] No doubt others are on the horizon, with these trends exemplifying the growing desires and needs among African diaspora and migrant churches amid a dynamic North American theological/educational landscape.

Transatlantic migration, however, pales compared to south-to-north migration from Central and South America. This has accounted for much of the above-mentioned Latinization of the Roman Catholic Church in the USA. In the first chapter I introduced the idea of the "evangelicalization" of theological education as a by-product of or phenomenon consistent with trends in North American Protestantism. Here, I need to be more precise about the character of this evangelical growth. The Assemblies of God, for instance, experienced over 13 percent growth between 2004 and 2014, but this was generated by cultural diversification and migration: the white adherents decreased by almost 2 percent during this time while nonwhites increased by over 43 percent.[10] Pew data provides more detailed analysis for the years 2007 to 2014: whites diminished from 72 to 66 percent while Latino/as increased from a tad under one-fifth to about one-fourth; even more drastically, within the close cousin pentecostal denominational group, the Church of God (Cleveland, Tennessee), whites decreased from 83 to 65 percent and Latino/as increased from 11 to 28 percent (Pew, 124). Latino/as have always been part of the pentecostal-evangelical milieu in North America, but these movements are now being buoyed even more visibly by migrants from Latin American countries.

Within Latino/a pentecostal-evangelical communities, however, educational currents diverge from what are found in the African American and African diaspora groups.[11] In part because of language differences but also because of the lack of distinctive institutional options (there are no "historically Hispanic" schools accredited by the ATS in mainland USA, for instance, although there are a few predominantly white seminaries that have Spanish-language programs and a few schools in Puerto Rico), the "pipeline" into ATS-related graduate level courses of study is more underdeveloped. Yet this not to say that there are no educational options, only that they are more grassroots, for many of them operate as institutes and certificate programs in the network of the Asociación para la Educación Teológica Hispana (AETH).[12] For instance, within the Latino/a Assemblies of God, dozens of Bible institutes have dotted the Pacific coast and Southwest states over the last century,[13] each with a unique profile, connected with others in these regions to some extent but autonomous in other respects, offering a variety of courses for personal enrichment but also a range of certificates of ministerial training and other "degrees" (many not formally accredited). For example, LABI College (formerly Latin American Bible Institute) now holds candidate status with the Association for Biblical Higher Education (ABHE) accrediting organization, which is a major step toward the highest level of accreditation in the future, and has both formal and informal relationships with these institutes, training laypersons, deacons, and ministers in these ecclesial communities at pretertiary domains on the one hand but, on the other, also providing college-level programs of study that facilitate graduate and alumni matriculation, on a contingent basis, into accredited postgraduate theological education.[14] This is paralleled by a different set of initiatives in the Roman Catholic Church, which serves a large Latino/a population but does so through tiered programs of theological education at parish, religious, diocesan, and other levels.[15]

South-north migration is linked with east-west migration,[16] especially since trans-Pacific flows were steady into Latin and South America prior to the Immigration and Nationality Act of 1965 that reopened portals into the USA from across the Asian continent. The growth of Christianity in South Korea over the last half of the previous century and the strong links between South Korean and American churches have generated at least seven Korean-language ATS-affiliated schools (representing Presbyterian, Evangelical Holiness, Baptist, and Methodist streams of Korean and Korean American Christianity, respectively), besides a handful of other programs in historically white seminaries with Korean-language programs across North America. Since China has begun to enter the global economy, we are now also seeing a growing number of Chinese-language schools. While clustered in California, these schools are spread around the country, with three ATS-accredited schools (all Taiwanese centered,[17] Baptist oriented, and conservative and evangelical in confession), one affiliated with the Asia Theological Association, five other fledgling endeavors, and another handful of Chinese-language programs of study in mostly white seminaries. The ongoing opening up of China to the rest of the world suggests that future demand for these courses of study will intensify rather than lessen, even as we may see other language-based schools and programs of study also emerge (like two Vietnamese seminaries in the greater Los Angeles area, one nondenominational and the other affiliated with the Christian and Missionary Alliance, which has a long history in Vietnam).

In sum: Theological education in North America will continue to flatten out due to migration and globalization trends. If the "browning" of the church across this continent involves not only its ongoing Latinization but also Africanization and Asianization, then the demands for theological education will stretch to include these contextual realities. These inter- and transcultural dynamics are also at the heart of the church and its educational tasks when we consider developments across world Christianity.

World Christianities: Education from Everywhere to Everywhere

Much as we are seeing North American interlinkages to the rest of the world, so too globalizing dynamics shifting our attention to these arenas help us to appreciate the horizontality of our interconnected world. At least three aspects of this "flattening" are important for our purposes.

First, the last half century has seen Christianity's center of gravity shift decisively from the Euro-American West to the Global South,[18] meaning that there have been, are now, and will continue to be many more Christians in Asia, Africa, and Latin America than in Europe and North America (where the majority of Christians resided from the year 500 to about 1950).

Second, the Protestant forms of this new "world Christianity," while in many respects reacting to the legacy of the colonial missionary enterprise, are evangelical in many significant respects, not least in their biblicism,[19] even if surely not in following strictly after the movement's North American institutional forms. Ironically, there are evangelical flows east-west and north-south that connect these churches, even as the baggage that has accrued to that label in the North American context has not carried over completely into the majority-world churches.

Third and most significantly for us, there is an undeniable pentecostalization and charismatization of these segments of world Christianity, in one respect owing to expansion of classical pentecostal movements, in another respect coming from charismatic renewal in the historic churches, and in a third respect related to the character of indigenous Asian, African, and Latin American spiritualities that map rather effortlessly onto pentecostal and charismatic sensibilities, practices, and inclinations.[20]

Flattening is thus occurring in terms of geographic expansion shifting the Christian center of gravity, of ecclesial democratization related to the evangelical emphasis on the priesthood of all believers and lay participation, and of charismatization of networks and relationships prominent within pneuma-centric churches and movements.

It must be granted that such "flattening" of the churches is brought about by the market forces at the heart of the network and information economy. To that extent, the church is as much a product of late modern capitalism as it is an expression of the body of Christ and the people of God. Similarly, by extension, theological education itself is caught up in the market flows of late capitalism, even as we can see the formation of consortia of theological institutions both anticipating and participating in these global processes of flattening and networking. So, on the one hand, we recognize that the church is an interim, dynamic, and organic body that heralds the coming reign of God precisely through recognition of its penultimacy that is intertwined with a world and its systems that are passing away; so also are institutions of theological education similarly carried at least in part by market flows (as chap. 5 later will detail). On the other hand, the outpouring of the Spirit promises to redeem the witness of this broken body in accordance with the promise of the gospel of Jesus Christ, and this buoys the hope that theological education can also participate in that redemptive work to the degree that it lifts up rather than enervates this gospel message.

But I am jumping ahead of myself. Our current discussion is focused on an increasingly evangelicalizing and pentecostalizing Christianity in a networked world. How is theological education understood when viewed in this globalizing context? Within the mainline Protestant churches, in particular those affiliated with the ecumenical umbrella organization the World Council of Churches (WCC), the trends have generally been toward a post-colonial orientation, one intentionally reactionary against the colonial legacy. Such churches and theological education institutions tend to emphasize interfaith dialogue, issues of gender and sexuality, and socioeconomic, political, and public theological concerns, among other matters central to ecumenically inclined churches.[21] As of early 2019, approximately thirty schools were affiliated with the Network of Institutions of Higher Ecumenical Theological Education (NIHETE), but this is only a fraction of those formerly connected with the World Conference of Associations of Theological Institutions (WOCATI), which represented the educational work of the WCC's Commission on Education and Ecumenical Formation, which mostly serves churches within more ecumenically leaning traditions. Within the scope of the broad spectrum of churches in the WCC orbit, there are literally thousands of Bible schools, institutes, and seminaries operating at different levels of development and accreditation.[22] Throughout, even if the laity of these Protestant churches around the world are often evangelical and pentecostal in piety and practice, many of these schools have historically been more ecumenical in character.

Yet, alongside institutional networks like NIHETE and WOCATI is also a more evangelical group, the International Council for Evangelical Theological Education (ICETE). This council is actually an umbrella organization derived from the World Evangelical Alliance's Theological Commission that includes nine regional or continental accrediting agencies covering (alphabetically) Africa (Association for Christian Theological Education in Africa), Asia (Asia Theological Association), the Caribbean (Caribbean Evangelical Theological Association), Europe (European Evangelical Accrediting Association), Euro-Asia (the Euro-Asian Accrediting Association), Latin America (Association for Evangelical Theological Education in Latin America), the Middle East and North Africa (Middle East Association for Theological Education), North America (Association for Biblical Higher Education), and the South Pacific (South Pacific Association of Evangelical Colleges). Excepting the schools in Europe and North America, there are over 504 institutes, colleges, seminaries, etc.—with over 100 of these in India and 90 in Brazil—that are either affiliated with or formally accredited by the ICETE groups in the Global South. If world Christianity is both evangelicalizing and pentecostalizing/charismatizing, then the developing expansiveness of such educational endeavors in the majority world should not be surprising.

To be sure, many of these evangelical schools in the majority world are relatively new and still developing, and hence do not yet operate at the level of ATS institutions in North America. If the Association for Biblical Higher Education (ABHE) in North America is considered a stepping-stone toward full ATS accreditation, in many ways theological education at least in the West has reached a level of maturity that remains largely aspired to around the world. The West has faculty, financial, capital, library, and other resources that far exceed what is available to most schools in the Global South. Evangelical seminaries and like institutions in Asia, Africa, and Latin America thus are often looking to partner with North American schools in order to benefit from the faculty expertise and other resources that they are struggling to develop. In that respect, globalization facilitates not just migration to North America but also a form of neocolonialism, at least in the educational sphere, in which Western institutions continue to set the standard for framing what theological education should look like. Theological educators in the so-called

Global North, then, ought to be cognizant that their efforts are often exported, even if they do not consciously teach for transnational consumption and implementation.

At the same time, reverse currents of influence are also now part of the mix. The evangelical and pentecostal/charismatic flavor of much of world Christianity, coupled with the migratory trends that characterize east-west and south-north movements, means that Asians, Africans, and Latin Americans are coming to Europe and North America, bringing their religious commitments with them and working out their missionary vocations along the way. This means that majority-world churches and theological institutions are laboring to develop missionary skills and evangelistic activities that can empower effective Christian witness to the ends of the earth, which lie for them in the Euro-American hemispheres.[23] If theological educators in the USA think they are training students only for missionary work in the classical sense of going abroad to Asia, Africa, and Latin America, their graduates will not know how to respond to the transformation of church and society effected by both migration and the so-called reverse missionary thrust of these majority-world diasporic and migrant churches.[24]

Thus, there is a gradual decentering of Western (European) normativity in the ongoing theological conversation. Where mainline Protestantism's more postcolonial sensibilities are being inculcated in ecumenical schools and institutions, the evangelical and pentecostal movements' cultural diversity and indigenous spiritualities are also manifesting in their churches and appearing in their programs of theological education. Since there is neither a pope nor a magisterium to dictate the way forward within the Protestant world, the flourishing of world Christianities in their distinctive ethnic and cultural forms coming from and going out in multiple and reciprocal directions means that theological education for the third millennium will have to be similarly and capably engaged if it is to serve the church catholic and its various peoples of God speaking in many tongues.

The Church at/from the Ends of the Earth: Pentecostalizing Theological Education

It is remarkable that only in the fairly recent past has Christianity finally become a *world religion*, one found almost literally in "every nation under heaven" (Acts 2:5). Yet there is a sense in which the beginnings of the church as people of God have always been inclusive of those at and from "the ends of the earth" (1:8). On the one hand, as Luke maps the Acts narrative, the story of early Christian and apostolic witness travels from Jerusalem, through "Judea and Samaria, and to the ends of the earth" (1:8), meaning that the advance of the gospel reaches and ends in Rome (Acts 28), the furthest region of the known world at that time from a Jerusalem-centric perspective. On the other hand, Luke also tells us that on the Day of Pentecost, when the new people of God are constituted through the outpouring of the Holy Spirit promised by Jesus (1:5, 8), there were present in the streets of Jerusalem "visitors from Rome, both Jews and proselytes" (2:10b), who were also, presumably, part of the three thousand baptized in response to the Pentecost message (2:41). The church goes out from Jerusalem to the world, even as the world is already gathered in Jerusalem.

There is a sense, then, in which Christianity has always been "global," from its beginnings to the present in the third millennium. The earliest messianists, of course, were "global," not in the sense understood now at the beginning of the twenty-first century—certainly not literally in a geographic manner as encompassing every nation and continent around the world, and surely not socially according to contemporary economic or digital linkages. Yet as Luke puts it, on the Day of Pentecost "there were devout Jews from every nation under heaven living in Jerusalem" (2:5), and he enumerates seventeen different groups of peoples (2:7–11) who were hearing the gathered crowd "speaking in the native language of each" (2:6b). This enumerated list is well known as Luke's much shorter version of the Old Testament's "table of seventy nations" that was supposed to cover the known world,[25] and the author of the book of Acts is clearly indicating that even if the entirety of the narrative to follow is supposed to disclose the trek of the gospel to the ends of that world, he understands and is attempting to communicate to his readers that the world is already there at the heart of the establishment of the fellowship of the Spirit as the new people of God.

The story of Acts is understood to cover the journey undertaken by the first generation of the church, concluding with Paul in Rome, prior to the destruction of Jerusalem in 70 CE. Within these first few decades, multiple centers of theological education emerge. Of course, Jerusalem, where the twelve apostles are, is a kind of originating point. It was from there that the apostolic teachings were originally dispensed (2:42). Yet even while the apostles are supposed to have primary responsibility for "the word of God" in this Jerusalemite community (6:2b), Hellenistic converts like Stephen and Philip, those from around the known Mediterranean world, end up becoming renowned spokespersons for the faith (Acts 6–7). They also become catalysts for the gospel moving beyond the local areas into Samaria and beyond (Acts 8). Later, the church at Antioch in Syria also appears to emerge as a center for theological teaching, and it seems to attract a rather diverse "faculty"—"prophets and teachers," Luke calls them (13:1a). The names and designations suggest a range of social and ethnic identities: "Barnabas [from Cyprus; 4:36a], Simeon who was called Niger, Lucius of Cyrene, Manaen a member of the court of Herod the ruler, and Saul" (13:1b).[26] The Saul referenced here is also the apostle Paul, and this verse launches his apostolic ministry, which includes, among other accomplishments, the establishment not only of a church but also of a kind of school at Ephesus in Asia Minor that ran for over two years (19:8–10). This later became the site of a distinguished teaching community gathered around at least the legacy of the apostle John, if not the historical man himself.[27] The final words of the book of Acts tell us both that the story has culminated at the ends of the earth, in Rome, as foreshadowed in the volume's table of contents (1:8), and that something like a Pauline school was in session: "He lived there two whole years at his own expense and welcomed all who came to him, proclaiming the kingdom of God and teaching about the Lord Jesus Christ with all boldness and without hindrance" (28:30–31).

The first generation of the church as the people of God also featured a plurality of centers for theological education and instruction, involving diverse leaders spread out across the face of the known world. This is what I call not just the church *after* Pentecost but also *theological education of and from Pentecost*, meaning that Luke gives us glimpses of the people of God teaching and learning variously not just after incarnation, resurrection, and ascension but also after Jesus's pouring out of the Spirit from the right hand of the Father (2:33) to and from the ends of the earth. Certainly, I am urging this perspective as a pentecostal theologian shaped by the modern pentecostal ecclesial experience, but I need to be clear that I am not so foolish as to suggest that Pentecostal denominational endeavors point the way forward for the next generation of theological education. Instead, I am making the theological argument that the body of Christ and the people of God have always also been the fellowship of the Spirit and hence exist in the light of Pentecost. By extension, if world Christianity in the twenty-first century is both evangelical and pentecostal/charismatic, it is so less in the modern pentecostal sense and more in the Lukan sense that the heart and soul of the people of God reverberate with the animation of the divine breath and wind poured out on the Day of Pentecost. Much as this event initiated the church into the redemptive mission of God, theological education after Pentecost also is caught up in this missional plan. If it is to have any hope of engaging and empowering the church as the people of God around the world, theological education must be renewed in, through, and by encountering that same Spirit.

Theological Transformation of the Church

Empowering the Fellowship of the Spirit

This first part of the book has focused on the church as one of the primary sites or publics for theological education, beginning in North America and broadening out to the rest of the world. Along the way we have begun to recognize that the body of Christ and the people of God are also, and always have been, the fellowship of the Spirit, those enabled and encouraged by the divine breath poured out on all flesh on the Day of Pentecost. Yet, just as that event elicited bewilderment, amazement, astonishment, and perplexity (Acts 2:6, 7, 11), so also do the ongoing and contemporary works of the divine wind provoke as much dissonance as consonance.[1] Movements of the Spirit are messy, and that is why, historically, Christendom, or the church institutional, has always privileged its hierarchical structures and attempted to control—if not marginalize, ignore, or reject—its charismatic impulses.[2] No wonder institutions of theological education struggle for spiritual renewal and vitality. Going forward, how might such entities be charismatically and pentecostally refreshed in their efforts to engage and serve churches as movements rather than as established structures amid the systems and hierarchies necessary for accredited education?

I sidestep this question for a moment to explore the presumed boundaries of the fellowship of the Spirit in relationship to the so-called nones and other hybridized forms of messianic discipleship, and then to consider how digital technologies are fostering virtual ecclesial communities that stretch the received definition of the body of Christ as incarnational reality. The third and final section of this chapter gathers up our ecclesial reflections and asks pointed questions about how the variegated forms of the contemporary *ekklēsia* pose both challenges to and opportunities for theological education. More precisely, it probes the implications of the dynamic character of the church as the heart and soul of theological education and considers the pressures these prompt. The transition from a hierarchical, authoritarian, elitist, and structured Christendom to a porous, organic, (digitally) networked, and experientially revitalized church both admonishes the status quo of theological education and charts pathways for effectively engaging the fellowship of the Spirit's present and discernible trends.

One important caveat needs to be reiterated before proceeding. I caution classical pentecostal adherents reading this book against the triumphalism that has often marked the movement's self-understanding.[3] In fact, not everything that calls itself pentecostal is necessarily part of the impending reign of God; the charismatic leader of a pentecostal megachurch can be far more authoritarian than the leadership of a Congregationalist, Baptist, Quaker, or other church that makes decisions as a "committee" of the whole. This is precisely why this chapter focuses on communities representative of the fellowship of the Spirit that are on the margins of (if affiliated at all with) modern pentecostal and charismatic movements. This is also an appropriate occasion to remind ourselves that our commitments are first and foremost to the Lukan narrative of the Pentecost outpouring and its early messianic effects rather than to the "success stories" of particular twentieth-century institutions that go by the (Pentecostal) name.

"Nones," Multiple-Religious Belongers, Insiders, and Others: Jesus Followers in 2020

The question of the nature of the church is so challenging today in part because its so-called borders are indistinct, both here in

North America and in the broader world. In the USA, the diminishing of mainline Protestantism and the growth of more evangelical expressions are, ironically, symptomatic of a larger social process that includes the palpable cultural triumph of mainline Protestantism's values: pluralism, emancipation, tolerance, free critical inquiry, as well as forms of individualism and experientialism that are also central to evangelical sensibilities.[4] Perhaps this same process gives rise to an emerging sociocultural segment that sociologists have come to describe as the "nones"—the religiously uncommitted, unaffiliated, or disengaged.

Here are some of the relevant considerations. A 2015 Pew survey, for instance, indicated that these "unaffiliated" increased from 16.1 percent of the total US population in 2007 to 22.8 percent in 2014. Of these, a little less than a third were either atheistic or agnostic, and almost a third said religion still remained important in some sense.[5] The latter group has also been identified in the literature as "apatheistic"—being believers in God but not engaged in formal or institutionally mediated religiosity—or as "spiritual but not religious," meaning they are not just unaffiliated but also have chosen not to associate with religious institutions in their ongoing religious or spiritual journey.[6] Almost eight in ten adults who identify as "nones" were raised religiously, including 28 percent as Catholics, 21 percent as mainline Protestants, and even 7 percent as evangelicals, compared to 21 percent who grew up without religious affiliation.[7] This tells us not only that the unchurched are largely the formerly churched but also that they may be spiritually active and perhaps even in their own way engaged in a relationship with God or Jesus Christ. (And even among the immigrant groups that currently may be keeping evangelical and pentecostal church attendance afloat, second and later generations of these groups are subject to similar pressures.) But even these qualifications mask the heterogeneity of these classifications, suitable for demographic purposes (perhaps) but not for any informed understanding of the spiritual and religious pluralism that characterizes these labels.[8]

This "spiritual but not religious" group is even more complicated when situated in a global context. In my own typology, I see two broad groups, one arguably within the church and the other clearly outside the church. Each group can be delineated triadically. Ecclesially speaking, there are, first, those who in some respects belong to or identify a congregation as their religious home, but not exclusively so—they also participate in other spiritual or religious activities, whether they frequent meditation halls that are more generic or even religiously affiliated or periodically consult indigenous healers or shamans or access other religious services for needs deemed unmet in their home religious context. Second are the "multiple religious belongers," primarily but not exclusively a Western and even North American phenomenon; these somehow claim either formal affiliation with two (or in rarer cases, more) religious traditions or are informally practitioners of the spiritual paths of more than one tradition.[9] Third are those who practice their faith in Israel's Messiah as Jesus devotees but do so within other religious communities, those "insider movements" that claim to nurture faith in Christ, albeit as part of Islamic, Hindu, or Buddhist social, cultural, and even institutional contexts.[10] The former two are clearly ecclesially active, however skeptical traditionalists might be of such definition, with insider movements just as evidently at best on the margins of the institutional church, with any defensible ecclesial claim viable only at the level of spiritual practice and pursuit. In short, the forms of the church considered across the spiritual marketplace are being stretched; just as important is that such religious and spiritual pursuits are occurring in ways that are inevitably generating new expressions of the church as the fellowship of the Spirit.

This trajectory of consideration is extended with a second group of spiritual seekers, those exploring options well outside traditional ecclesial domains.[11] Within this sphere are, first, the spiritual seekers who are looking for meaning and fulfillment anywhere but in institutionally related Christian expressions; second, spiritualists who are indifferent not just to institutional Christianity but to any other institutionally organized form of religiosity; and third, agnostics or atheists who, while questioning or rejecting belief in traditional notions of deity, are nevertheless, in their own self-understanding, spiritually attuned and invested persons. The point is that the "spiritual but not religious" come in many types.[12] Just as important if not more so for our purposes, even if such persons might not be interested in institutional or ecclesial forms of Christian faith, they are often spiritually engaged both in the private sphere and in the workplace.[13]

We might think that theological education ought to be focused on equipping the church and its members who are interested in faithful Christian living, and so wonder why we should worry about those on the margins or outside of historically defined ecclesial communities. We should be concerned for these people because traditional notions of the church are no longer dominant. If the first chapter showed that denominational structures are being displaced by fluid networks, and the second indicated that such networks are being reconfigured globally by transnational migration and intercultural interaction, then here we see how a growing number of people are not interested in the church but may be spiritually active and even open to being introduced to and relating with Jesus in spiritually vibrant ways. What are the implications of this for the church? For theological education? How do we engage such a potential audience that may be interested in a theological course of study as part of their spiritual quest? Is this what we want or need to consider? If so, how might such connections be forged, and toward what ends?

Millennials and Digital Culture: Spiritualities in a Networked Twenty-First Century

In a flat world, links are pervasively digitally mediated. The millennial generation, those born between 1977 and 1995, is the "first digitally savvy generation."[14] Coming close on the heels of these millennials, members of the so-called Generation Z (those born after 1996) are getting their own smart phones in their early teenage years.[15] These trends are only going to deepen when considered in global context. Even with various constraints and inequality of access, Africa, the youngest continent in the world, with six out of every ten persons being under the age of twenty-five,[16] boasts countries with up to 70 percent of the people on the Internet, "mostly on mobile phones."[17]

This level of digital existence and mediation, in large part facilitated through mobile devices, is part of what some call "Web 3.0."[18] If Web 1.0 was the primordial Internet with email capacity, and 2.0 included social media and other activity facilitating mass collaborative creation of web content, then 3.0 involves innovations like cloud computing that enable access and portability, smart platforms that allow for interactivity across programs and digital software, and handheld devices that facilitate mobility and constant connectivity. There is a flatness of interconnectedness at the level of individuals, then, that involves relational selves participating on individualized networks that in turn provide various senses of collective sociality in these various digital domains.

What does this mean for religion in a digital and networked world? Some traditional churches have already migrated online and have a digital or virtual presence. At a minimum, church websites provide information that allows seekers to become acquainted with their churches and, if so inclined, visit in person. Some congregations, however, are doing much more, innovatively engaging in ecclesial work via electronically mediated forums. Services are not just archived for later review but also increasingly simulcast live to allow "participation" from a distance for those unable or unwilling to attend in person. Some say that even the Eucharist can be given and taken online.[19] Pastoral activity is also increasingly offered via digital means, whether in daily readings, prayers, and words of encouragement or in personalized "chat" or related forums that allow for consultation (pastoral counseling, traditionally). Churches alert to the growing numbers of unchurched persons have also been asking how to engage in evangelistic and other missional activities via the Internet so as to reach those unaffiliated with traditional congregations.[20] The lines between the real and the online or virtual church are in some respects increasingly blurred.

The development of Second Life and related online worlds has led to the formation of wholly virtual religious communities, including not just Christian groups but almost every other faith tradition that comes to mind. Millennials and others who are looking for egalitarian and democratic rather than authoritarian and hierarchical social spaces, who are looking for freedom of expression beyond the rule-based religiosity of their upbringing, or who are seeking what they believe to be more authentic forms of spirituality and relationality are increasingly finding these spaces, religious expressions, and relationships online.[21] These virtual religious communities connect people from around the world and are providing them outlets for exploring and constructing the kind of holistic spirituality for which they are looking. This is one reason why the traditional call to mission is migrating online: not only is it costly in time and resources to be a missionary in the historic sense, but it is also less politically correct, especially for white Americans, to go to regions in the Global South when those parts of the world are sending as many or even more "missionaries"—often among those defined as immigrants—to the West. Positively put, however, members from any and virtually (pun intended) every religious tradition can be evangelists online, "inhabiting" various cyberspaces where they can meet people of any faith or no faith at all and share their "good news." In short, religion is thriving electronically, both in its traditional expressions of connecting those with like spiritual interests and in facilitating digital forms of religious proselytism.

Online spirituality and religiosity are neither transcendently spiritual nor immanently historical, meaning that the digital medium is facilitating real interpersonal exchanges that both transcend human beings around the world and also connect flesh-and-blood creatures whenever and wherever they are "plugged in."[22] Yes, perhaps for those more traditional, the electronic medium entails much more preliminary work before face-to-face meetings "seal the deal" religiously, so to speak. On the other side, religion is just as "real" online as it is off; in fact, for many people the digital realm may be the only dimension through which they are religious practitioners. Besides, such religious forums are attractive not only for the "spiritual but not religious" or "multiple religious belonging" groups; the digital world allows for the commingling of these with others in the forging of cybernetic religiosity.

Against this backdrop, it is not surprising that higher education in general and theological education itself is migrating onto the online platform.[23] I am not sure there are any theological schools left that are not utilizing the digital medium in some way, even as many are now offering fully online graduate-level programs, including the master of divinity degree. Thinking about online theological education should not merely be about translating what is done in regular classrooms onto the digital platform. Instead, the connectivist and constructivist world of the Internet requires, effectively, a wholly rethought philosophy and theology of education. Indeed, in a "flat" world that is electronically mediated, we are having to reconsider church, community, and education simultaneously. It is not that traditional brick-and-mortar theological institutions are disappearing into the digital realm— although some schools are emerging that operate only in online modalities—but that education is increasingly open via the Internet. This requires theological educators to ask hard questions about engaging the fellowship of the Spirit in this domain.[24]

Beyond "Us" and "Them"? Spirit-izing/Practicing Theological Education

So, what exactly is the heart and soul of theological education becoming? Grassroots ecclesial forms are gradually displacing the Christendom that birthed theological education as we currently understand it. Independent networks of relational bodies are flattening hierarchical denominations, while migration and globalization are prompting new links and connections across national, cultural, and other boundaries. Whereas previously we equated the church with its institutional and denominational underpinnings, the trend today is to recognize that the church as the fellowship of the Spirit is defined organically, interpersonally, and relationally, even according to Jesus's words from two thousand years ago: "where two or three are gathered in my name, I am there among them" (Matt. 18:20), no matter if these two or three are congregationally unaffiliated (spiritual but not religious), participants in multiple religious paths, or practicing their faith in Jesus while being members of other religious communities. People are hungry for significant spiritual experiences and meaningful religious lives, and will receive them if available from "churches" of whatever form, but they are less inclined to look for these in established and institutionally expansive structures.

It is of little surprise that theological education in the Christendom mode is just as hierarchical as the form of the church that gave it birth. Graduate theological education, after all, is a thoroughly elitist enterprise, serving only those who already have at least an undergraduate degree, and this is consistent with the layered church that has historically elevated clergy *over* laity.[25] But in the increasingly flat world that we are inhabiting, a modality of education accessible only to a select few will not serve the lifeblood that runs through the church's most vital veins. Ethnic minorities, immigrants and migrants, majority-world ecclesial adherents and members, those spiritual but not religious or those spiritual and multiply religious, the "nones," and many other so-called ecclesial outliers may be interested in theological education but would not be able to matriculate. The answer is not to eliminate graduate-level theological programs but for leaders to reconsider how their work serves the plural and diverse church.

The Internet both intensifies and in some respects exacerbates the democratization of the twenty-first-century church. There is something about the christologically understood image of the body of Christ that calls attention to its embodied historicity. The church understood in terms of the physicality of its members invites what might be called an incarnational modality of theological education and formation, one that occurs in the interpersonal materiality of teachers and learners interacting with each other. Churches around the world and theological education that serves the heart and soul of the church also should be incarnational in some fundamental ways.

On the other hand, the church understood as the fellowship of the Spirit (2 Cor. 13:13) depends on the outpouring of the Spirit on *all* flesh (Acts 2:17), and this inspiration and enablement touches bodies through many venues. Without taking anything away from the physicality of apostolic missionary ventures and the planting of churches, we must say that early Christian leaders also exercised spiritual authority and oversight over these fledgling congregations and communities through a variety of modes, including, prominently, epistolary ones.[26] These letters and other texts (now collected in our New Testament) were media of instruction, exhortation, admonition, and shepherding from a distance. Today's electronic capacities eliminate the much longer time spans between sending and receiving over great distances. I am not arguing that we can shift completely into a digital format without losing something important and even essential to authentic Christian formation; I am suggesting that digitality in and of itself is not a threat to theological education and can even be a necessary (if not sole) medium.

I am likewise suggesting that the work of the Spirit that was formerly carried by apostolic letters can also be accomplished in the information age through electronic portals.[27] A church that is democratically linked through charismatically charged and experientially rich complexes invites theological education that can course through such nexuses; similarly, a church that is globally interconnected through electronic networks invites theological education that can flow through such nodes. The question to ask today is: What is the Spirit doing in and through the church? And how is the church becoming and being transformed in and through the power of the Spirit? This is not to baptize any empirical trend or actuality among what we call *church* as a purveyor of the Spirit's work, since much that goes on in the name of church does not attend to Jesus's message regarding the coming divine reign. But before we turn in the next part of this book to understanding further the rule of God that is normative for Christian discernment, we ought first to acknowledge that this rule of God comes about also through encountering and following the Spirit of Jesus. Hence we can provisionally say that a theological education undiscerning of the vitality of the Spirit's work cannot serve the body of Christ and people of God well, just as theological education unattentive to the dynamic character of the fellowship of the Spirit will not be a purveyor of renewal that is coming.

Theological education that is Spirit-ized and spiritually energized will be renewed to serve all flesh, just as incarnation and the Pentecost outpouring facilitated the rule and reign of God. Such a reconceptualized initiative has the potential to overcome the many divisions between "us" and "them." It is not, for instance, that the lines between "graduate" and "undergraduate" will no longer pertain, but that theological education will feed these mutually and, in some respects, reciprocally, reaching even "underneath" such levels to engage the church that is not so divided. Surely, we will need to think in, through, and beyond "West" and "rest"; in, through, and beyond "North" and "South"; in, through, and beyond "haves" and "have-nots"; in, through, and beyond "white" and "black" and "brown" and "yellow"; in, through, and beyond "able" and "disabled"; in, through, and beyond "insiders" and "outsiders"; in, through, and beyond the "nones" and the "somes"; in, through, and beyond spiritual (or not) and religious (or not); in, through, and beyond Christianity and other faiths; in, through, and beyond the church and the world; in, through, and beyond the incarnational and the digital; and so on. This is not to discard these categories completely but to think through how they have been reified in ways that may be both unhelpful (at best) and confusing (at worst) in a flat world.

We have covered a lot of ground in this first part, raising many questions along the way. Some readers might wish that some concrete "answers" had been included, at least to alleviate the sense of being overwhelmed by the complexity of the issues—although on this point I need to repeat that my goal is not to provide a "three-step solution" to our existing challenges. I have already begun to show how we can think pneumatologically about the church, and this itself anticipates our goal of developing a pneumatological imagination to grapple later with the task of theological education. But before we get to that, we must further ask: If theological education is to serve a church that is continuously becoming in our midst, toward what is such becoming directed or drawn? If part 1's question about the heart and soul of theological education shone the spotlight on the actual if ever-changing forms of the church that is the body of Christ and fellowship of the Spirit, part 2 asks about the hands and work of this diverse and organic people of God, whose burden decreases in proportion to the appearance of God's coming reign.

2

Witness in Glocal Contexts

The Hands and Works of Theological Transformation

4

Missional Information

Publicizing the Coming Age

The church, for all its dynamic variety, is an interim vehicle directed toward the new creation. What does it mean for theological education that its task is to nurture its heart and soul toward a transcendent horizon? How can theological education equip a diverse church for a mission that eventually should have no need for the church?

Rather than imprison the work of the church in the immanent and historical frame, I suggest a theological praxis through which the church collectively and its members individually manifest in diverse contexts, varied directions, and concrete practices the Spirit's ushering in of the coming reign (or kingdom) of God. Theological education is or should be devoted to participating in the rule of God by practicing the mission of God apparent in the incarnation and perpetuated through Pentecost. Admittedly, that formulation is rather abstract and general, but the outlines are clear in the gospel narratives and reinforced by the Acts account.[1] I have already suggested that this participation in the reign of God happens in the public sphere, the socioeconomic realm, and the interpersonal dimension. This holistic missiological vision is one in which individuals participate as ecclesially embedded rather than as solitary selves, but also as nested within existing political and socioeconomic systems. I can ask the question about theological education another way: What difference ought theological education to make for practical Christian faithfulness not *of* but *in* and *for* this world?

We begin to explore this mission by focusing on the political arena, broadly understood.[2] I explore the hands and works of the church first as manifest in the polis—meaning our human commons generally, not just the city-state—and then situate the mission of God's people within the broader terrestrial environment of our cosmic habitat. I conclude by sketching a rationale for theological education focused on this public and political-economic dimension in conversation with the apostolic example provided especially by the Lukan narratives. It is the question of *how* theological education can be better equipped for its *why*, or mission. For I join the chorus of voices insisting that the revitalization of theological education is inherently interlocked with the renewal of the missional efforts of the church,[3] but I also deepen this claim, given the world's connected, pluralistic, and cosmopolitan matrices. Many responses are needed for the Spirit's work to announce and actualize the coming rule of God. Might theological education be up to this task as renewed by that same Spirit?

Glocal Citizenship: Participating in the Reign of God

We begin with glocal citizenship, since our recognition of the church's diversity of expressions is correlated with our awareness that identity, including ecclesiality, is interrelationally, internationally, and ecumenically defined. Ecclesiology and polis are interconnected via migrating diasporas and transnational linkages. Church and society are mutually defining: both are local and yet global in different senses. The difference has to do with their telos or goal, and for the church this requires its full embrace of a fleeting identity and character that foresee the rule of God to come. How might theological education participate in empowering the mission of the church toward the coming divine reign, toward a time when ecclesial witness shall be transformed into the worship of the people of God gathered around the throne of the Lamb and the seven spirits?

To ask about the church's mission in this way may prompt retrievals of bygone images related to mass crusades and their associated "conversions" or to the forms of the so-called managerial missiology perceived as at least in part enumeratively motivated—counting how many churches planted, how many attendees at services, how many water baptisms, or how many evidences of Spirit baptism with its concomitant evidence of tongues speaking, etc. These are debated within the field of missiology,[4] but what is less objectionable is that remnants of colonial- and Christendom-forged missiological forms are increasingly less warrantable now.[5] Denominationally organized mission enterprises that send (usually Caucasian) missionaries from the West to the non-West are almost implausible in a migrating and digitally interconnected world. We have to reimagine the church's participation in the mission of God.

More than this, incarnational mission resulting in the Word of God made flesh and pentecostal witness involving the Spirit of God poured out on all flesh means that the saving work of the triune God is as much concerned with physicality, creatureliness, historicity, and sociality as with the earlier missiological foci. The bifurcation presumed in the prior message is now less presumed. As important is that ongoing scriptural scholarship highlight both the *now* and the *not-yet* of the next world in the present aeon. The church's eschatological witness is not about a transhistorical or otherworldly spiritualized time but hastens today what is still ahead of us and announces now that the time has already arrived at least in a preliminary manner through Christ by the power of the Spirit. This means that theological education must be relevant socially, politically, and economically.

Liberation theological discourses emerging out of late 1960s Latin America captured such this-worldly relevance of the gospel's transformative message, proclaiming that the good news of Jesus Christ interrogated, subverted, and called for the reconstitution of the systems and structures of this world. In many respects, this word had to be spoken with a kind of decisiveness in order to break the hold of otherworldliness on the missiological imagination: one often has to swing the pendulum all the way to the other side to find a *via media*.[6] The resulting conversation has indeed mediated the articulation of a more holistic missiological witness, one that is attentive to the spiritual in its material embeddedness and that recognizes the work of the triune God as encompassing past, present, and future.[7] Among evangelicals, the liberationist motif has been woven into a more fully orbed soteriological vision so that *misión integral*—integral or holistic mission—includes and involves the church's word and deed both to individuals for their personal "salvation" and to the world at large for the renewal of society in its various domains.[8]

The late David Bosch portended some of these ideas when over a quarter-century ago his portrait of the "emerging ecumenical missionary paradigm" included evangelism and the quest for justice next to one another.[9] Bosch's "mission as action in hope" also attempted to formulate an eschatological missiology whose horizons stretched from the cross and Pentecost to the parousia.[10] It is in this spatiotemporal middle place and time that the church's witness resounds to both individuals and the wider polis. Yes, evangelism has a personal character to it, inviting listeners to respond to the gospel's call to follow after the way of Jesus; but yes, evangelism also has social, political, and public dimensions, inviting communities to live out their discipleship on Jesus's way that has relevance for marginalized groups, vulnerable children, oppressed peoples, and civic and social spaces currently under the sway of destructive principalities and powers.[11] The church exists to announce the impending arrival of the rule of God, and this has implications for individual hearts, for local communities, and for the world's societies that God loves and wishes to renew and redeem.

What does this mean for theological education? This is fundamentally a missiological question: how to enable discernment of and then engagement with the world within which the church is called to bear witness. More to the point: if theological education is not neutral but *either* assimilates us into and preserves the status quo *or* liberates us from the world's fallen and unjust character,[12] then along the latter trajectory the missiological now also includes the redemptive transformation of the public and the political. Hence, missiology intersects with and is constituted partly by public theology and political theology.[13] It requires not just skills to steer through such plurality but a certain commitment to embracing pluralism as both a missional and a political project.[14]

The goal, however, cannot just be a reduction of theology to the political, as if theological education merely needed to become politicized. Theological schools are not in the business of training political scientists; that is another discipline with its own experts and expertise. Instead, the task is the more delicate one of nurturing a glocal Christian faithfulness and identity, one oriented toward the coming rule of God that is yet lived out in the present polis. This is life in Christ by the power of the Spirit that bears witness in the present space-time cosmopolis.[15]

That is, in fact, precisely the point of messianic discipleship portrayed in the early Christian community. Luke situates the entirety of the Jesus story, as well as that of his followers, amid the Pax Romana, under the rule and reign of earthly Caesars: Augustus and Tiberius (Luke 2:1; 3:1).[16] Both the gospel and the sequel, the Acts of the Apostles, are politically implicated, and the apostolic witness hence can also be received as representative of how that mission was politically explicated. Attending to the political framing of the apostolic narrative helps us to see how Spirit-empowered pentecostal witness engages the polis.[17] The church's mission is to publicize the rule and reign of God glimpsed in Jesus Christ by the power of the Spirit and thereby to enable prophetic discipleship between and beyond the partisanships that divide the church and paralyze Christian witness.

Cosmic Renewal: Tarrying at the Throne of God

If the missiological imagination remains focused only on the otherworldly task of saving souls from the devouring inferno that some believe is coming, the church will have failed to bear faithful witness and will be a bearer of words that baffle those who currently need and want to hear good news. The message about soul salvation cannot ignore the material and created order. For Gen Z, whether or not the world will eventually burn is moot since, as a by-and-large post-Christian group, they are confronted daily with the implications of climate change and feel betrayed by their elders' lack of will to discipline human consumption or enact environmentally sustainable practices and behaviors.[18]

But if the church's witness ought to be redirected from the former message of apocalyptic gloom and doom, then it must also learn to interact respectfully with other philosophies and ideologies that, while also devoted to ecological preservation, derive from very different sources and wisdom traditions. Neopagans, Gaia advocates, and indigenous people groups around the world have long been calling attention to the need to see human beings as intricately intertwined with the material environment, but their fundamental sensibilities are not always compatible with gospel commitments. Further, environmentalists and those working in the ecological and geophysical sciences are also dedicated to what some Christians today call creation care,[19] but again, their starting points are not the same as those for whom Jesus Christ is Lord. The reality is that the colonial enterprise already tried to wed the gospel to a certain set of culturally contrived values, and the result was bad news for non-Western peoples.[20] Our task now is not to exchange one set of culturally developed formulations for another, but to inhabit more deeply the call of the gospel in all contexts and to do so in ways that respectfully interact with our discussion partners, whether from religious and wisdom traditions or scientific and scholarly disciplines.

On the one hand, then, Christian witness as dialogue retrieves scriptural traditions that can enable collaborative and cooperative work for the flourishing of all creation that announces the coming rule of God. What comes to mind is the Isaianic heralding of when

a spirit from on high is poured out on us,
>and the wilderness becomes a fruitful field,
>and the fruitful field is deemed a forest.
Then justice will dwell in the wilderness,
>and righteousness abide in the fruitful field.
The effect of righteousness will be peace,
>and the result of righteousness, quietness and trust
>>forever.
My people will abide in a peaceful habitation,
>in secure dwellings, and in quiet resting places.

(32:15–18)[21]

Passages like this prompt questions regarding the prophetic vision of shalom, and how that involves the righting of injustices done to humans and to the wider creation.

On the other hand, Christian witness as liturgical is resourced from other texts and empowers faithful worship that heralds the coming reign of God. The final book of the Christian canon encourages missional witness that envisions both human participation in the worship of creation, the entirety of creation, before the throne of God (Rev. 4–5) and eternal worship in a new Jerusalem constituted also by a refurbished garden and renewed creation.[22] Christian dialogue and worship—both missional activities—are part and parcel of humanity's relating to God in its brokenness, yearning for the redemption to come. Saint Paul says that these prayers are also pneumatically generated: "We know that the whole creation has been groaning in labor pains until now; and not only the creation, but we ourselves, who have the first fruits of the Spirit, groan inwardly while we wait for adoption, the redemption of our bodies" (Rom. 8:22–23). Our tarrying in the Spirit through prayer and worship is part of the creation's own groaning at the divine footstool. The God enthroned on the seventh day is also the one who has sent his Son and poured out his Spirit to restore a world so it can be fully and wholly creation.

What I am after here is in part an environmental missiology that is also simultaneously a deeper and wider specification of

57

a public or political missiology.[23] Yet my goal here is not public, political, or environmental engagement for its own sake, but genuinely theological education that is directed toward the coming divine rule. The question is how theological education inspires Christian discipleship in a networked world of many voices and amid a polis of many agendas, many of which are important. Why? In a flat world, concerns about human interconnectedness, including environmental situatedness, cannot be ignored or dismissed. Hence, what we need is not just the ABCs of such an environmental or ecological theology but a broader theological frame for how to take up such considerations. This leads to our missiological vision: Toward what ends does theological education direct the work of ecclesial hands?

Theological education in the twenty-first century must enable not just glocal citizenship but also cosmic citizenship. Here I mean equipping Jesus followers for terrestrial habitation appropriate for many different glocal contexts with different issues and needs, yet still always as a mode of participating in the inaugurating work of the new Jerusalem. On the one hand, then, theological education empowers the differentiated works of ecclesial hands for the sake of the polis and of the world understood as the creation of God; on the other hand, theological education nurtures the full range of doxological practices—the patient and persistent praying and worshiping of ecclesial hearts—that yearns for the transformation of the polis and the cosmos as the inhabitation of the triune God.[24] Terrestrial citizenship is temporary but also anticipatory of heaven touching Earth. Orientation toward the coming divine rule does not bypass the need for earthly relevance even if the former is irreducible to the latter.

Apostolic Witness: Heralding the Rule of God

The question this chapter asks is how to recognize the church, given its horizontalization across the global and digital information economy. My preliminary response is that we discern the church's presence and activity insofar as such manifest the work of the Spirit poured out by Christ to usher in the reign of God. What and who the church is, in other words, can be revealed only by her deeds reflecting the arrival of the divine rule proclaimed by Jesus. In his own way, each of the gospel writers announces Jesus's commitment to the *basileia tou theou*—literally: *the kingdom of God*, or (less kyriarchically and less patriarchally) *the reign/rule of God*. Saint Luke's account involves Jesus's appeal to and quotation from the prophet Isaiah:

> "The Spirit of the Lord is upon me,
>> because he has anointed me to bring good news to
>> the poor.
> He has sent me to proclaim release to the captives
>> and recovery of sight to the blind,
>> to let the oppressed go free,
> to proclaim the year of the Lord's favor."
>
> (Luke 4:18–19; cf. Isa. 61:1–2a)

While Jesus's preaching of "the year of the Lord's favor" technically announces that the Levitical year of Jubilee is imminent, it also more generally anticipates that Yahweh will not put off forever ushering in the *basileia*, and the rest of the Third Gospel confirms through Jesus's words and deeds that his life and ministry are part and parcel of the *basileia tou theou*.

Remember that all of Jesus's edicts regarding the *basileia* occur amid the Pax Romana ruled not by Yahweh but by Caesar, and that he continued to emphasize this message about the divine rule even after his resurrection (Acts 1:3). It is not surprising then that even the disciples have a hard time comprehending that the messianic inauguration of the reign of God did not (at least not right away) involve overthrowing Roman rule in Palestine—so much so that in the moments before Jesus's ascension to heaven they are still wondering: "Lord, is this the time when you will restore the kingdom to Israel?" (1:6). Jesus's reply, intriguingly, does not deny the advent of the *basileia*, indicating only that the specific timing remains with the Father (1:7). More importantly, in this context messianic faithfulness amid the Pax Romana involves the coming of the Spirit: "But you will receive power when the Holy Spirit has come upon you; and you will be my witnesses in Jerusalem, in all Judea and Samaria, and to the ends of the earth" (1:8). The promised Spirit's outpouring that Luke details in the next chapter is a divine asset given both for political discipleship and for eschatological witness. As Luke recounts Peter's explanation drawn from the prophet Joel, the pentecostal gift is amid and for "the last days," initiating "the coming of the Lord's great and glorious day" (2:17a, 20b; cf. Joel 2:28–31). In sum, the apostolic witness is both political and eschatological simultaneously, not one or the other.

In the next chapter, I will discuss further the economic ramifications of the church's public and political witness. For the moment, however, we explore the idea that the apostolic participation in the mission of the Spirit involves the polis in the broad sense. Whereas the New Testament sometimes starkly contrasts the *church* with the *world*, at other times the church is constituted, at least in part, but essentially rather than parenthetically, by the nations. Thus, on the Day of Pentecost Luke is explicit that "there were devout Jews from every nation under heaven living in Jerusalem" (Acts 2:5), and that it was "Jews and proselytes" (2:10b) from across this first-century global (Mediterranean) world who were called by the gospel and initiated through baptism in Jesus's name (2:38) into the messianic community. The Spirit's renewing and revitalizing work, then, transpires in and through the peoples and nations of a world defined by the Roman imperial regime.

In the rest of Acts, the disclosing of the Spirit's empowered witness happens educationally in contexts that repeatedly involve the polis and ongoing proclamation of the *basileia tou theou*. The prophets and teachers gathered at Antioch included "Manaen a member of the court of Herod the ruler" (13:1), and it was out of this spirited and hybrid community that the apostolic mission to the ends of the Greco-Roman world was launched (13:2–4). Later, in Corinth, Saint Paul spent over two years "argu[ing] persuasively about the kingdom of God" in synagogues and lecture halls (19:8–10). Last but not least, at the end of the book (and also at the ends of the known world from a Jerusalem-centric perspective), the apostle Paul spends another two years in Rome evangelizing and "proclaiming the kingdom of God and teaching about the Lord Jesus Christ with all boldness and without hindrance" (28:31). The apostolic teaching, preaching, and evangelism enabled by the Spirit poured out at Pentecost involve instruction regarding the *basileia tou theou* that empowers the church's witness to and mission in the first-century cosmopolis.

By what, then, ought the heart and soul of theological education be captivated? By nothing less than the work of the reign of God, sustained by the Spirit of Jesus. If we are what we love, and if we are inhabited by the messianic Spirit that inaugurated the *basileia* two thousand years ago, then our loves will be oriented to the rule of God.[25] Such orientation is manifest in missional practices that make present but wait patiently for and proclaim the arrival of the divine reign. Yet our objective is neither merely to politicize theological education nor inappropriately to theologize the polis. Rather, the need in a democratically constituted global and connected world is for the *who* and *why* of theological education to be carefully calibrated so that we are clearer about how to orient the fellowship of the Spirit amid the many competing voices amplified in the third millennium. That is the nature of terrestrial evolution: that the church is less a hierarchically organized institution and more a hybrid and connectively constituted organism. Unless we can discern the form of the coming divine reign, who we are and what we pursue will be pulled incoherently in many directions.

Note, though, that the Pentecost outpouring means that it is not the plurality of voices, languages, cultures, and identities that is the issue, since the particularity of the many tongues and their concomitant practices are valued and heard (see Acts 2:6, 11b) rather than unheeded or muzzled. Consequently, the many tongues magnified across the twenty-first-century polis also should not, pneumatologically and pentecostally understood, be a problem. This is not a politically correct multiculturalism but a theologically and missiologically funded pluralism for the sake of the justice of the coming reign of God. Spirited theological education hence will welcome, augment, and expand the many theoretical perspectives and practical expressions since the coming *basileia tou theou* will include those "from every tribe and language and people and nation" (Rev. 5:9b). More pointedly, we need the many voices resonating in the cosmic cosmopolis because they bring with them many practices and capacities to resonate with the rule and reign of God in many glocal contexts.[26]

5

Market Reformation

Materializing the Jubilee Spirit

In this chapter, I look at these many public and political voices through an economic lens. For not only does the *basileia tou theou* have an economic or Jubilee dimension, but the current crisis of theological education is often perceived by leaders as first of all an economic crisis. In a glocal and connected world, the economic register is interwoven with that of the polis at large, and hence is also integral to any discussion of the health of the church's heart and soul, hands and work. To grapple adequately with the *why* of the church's commitments requires confronting and getting over the economic hurdles.

Yet, our engagement with the world, including its economics, cannot be on the terms set out by economists. Theological educators are not so trained and so should not presume to be economically competent. However, we ought to listen to the witness of economists and seek the Spirit's interpretation of their "tongues" for our theological purposes. While affordability and sustainability are essential matters, any theological education that is driven primarily by these concerns will be less theologically compelled and missiologically oriented and will instead become increasingly indistinguishable from any other educational commodity.

The three parts of this chapter attempt to grapple with the economic dilemma confronting contemporary theological education, then outline ways in which theological schools have begun responding to and engaging with this dilemma, and finally resituate the economic within the theological and missiological horizon, especially the *basileia tou theou* toward which the church is working. If in the preceding chapter our focus was on the various theological practices of intercommunally embodying the divine reign in our meeting together, worship, and witness, here the focus is on the ecclesial posture of generosity and the missional practices of sharing. On the one hand, some of what we will be discussing considers ways in which theological schools prepare learners for mission-driven engagement with the economy, but the more important aspects of our exploration focus on the economic life of theological institutions and the ways in which they ought to engage and operate missionally within the contemporary market economy. If theological educators can embrace the many voices of the Spirit, then not only will their courses of study more effectively discipline theological learners in cosmopolitan and glocal contexts but their practices—the hands of theological education—will also be normed by the coming divine economy of abundance and sharing. This chapter hence provides a central (economic) link mediating political and personal witness that participates in the divine economy and is reoriented missionally to the *basileia tou theou*.

Late Modern Capitalism: Commercializing Divinity

Any frank assessment of contemporary theological education will acknowledge that steep economic challenges are forcing closure of schools and leading to mergers of institutions and other drastic measures (like selling of property and even relocation) in attempts to secure financial stability. I begin by recapping and making more explicit some of the pressures, but this time from an economic perspective.

Denominational demands for credentialed clergy that drove

much of the market for theological education during the first half of the prior century have eroded significantly and show no signs of rebounding. The previous era's gold-standard master of divinity that presumed an undergraduate degree is both less meaningful in a postdenominational world and largely out of reach for broad segments of the "brown church" that are barely beginning tertiary educational endeavors. More and more college graduates who desire to pursue further study in theology are entering graduate studies with higher and higher levels of educational debt. To increase that debt yet further at the postgraduate level is unjustifiable, since the market for such degrees does not promise salaries adequate to repay such obligations. Even worse, starting in 2025, a sharp decline in high school graduates is predicted,[1] and this will diminish the number of traditional college-age students, which will also reduce the pool of graduate learners, at least of those in their midtwenties. Last but by no means least, the economic recession of 2008–2009 did much to deplete whatever meager endowments some theological institutions had, thus escalating tuition dependency and undermining even more the affordability of this level of study.

The growth of Christianity across the majority world is surely increasing demands for theological education in global contexts. Theological schools in the Global South, however, are having to build from the ground up, starting with basic certificates for those without even high school diplomas. Even if the latter could be presumed, the explosive growth of the church in these regions means that practical ministerial training is an urgent priority and graduate-level sophistication a distant commitment. Further, as noted above, the most vital Christian communities are frequently of the evangelical and pentecostal sort, and their histories include a substantial anti-intellectual strain that is generally suspicious of theological education and more pragmatically inclined. To compound matters, Christian growth accelerating across the majority world, especially in economically developing regions, means that the widening economic disparities in these contexts map onto what is happening in churches and their theological education efforts, so that the chasm separating endeavors in the Global South from those in the West seems to be broadening rather than narrowing.

Of course, theological education has tried to adjust. Aside from some of the more drastic measures, schools have attempted to increase tuition revenue especially through overhauling the curriculum, eliminating underenrolled programs (and thereby also downsizing as deemed appropriate), developing new certificates and programs of study, launching online modalities to engage nonlocal learners or others looking for greater flexibility of study options, and relying more and more on adjunct, part-time, and other non-tenure-track or contingent faculty. Additional efforts to generate tuition income include forming agreements with undergraduate programs to secure academic trajectories for students who wish to build toward a graduate theological degree, targeting adult or second-career students who may be interested in theological education later in life, and shoring up retention of matriculated students. Many theological institutions also have embarked on strenuous cost-cutting initiatives, streamlined operations, centralized administrative functions, and purged duplication and inefficiencies toward being fiscally leaner organizations. There are also an increasing number of collaborations, consolidations, and partnerships, not least the outsourcing of services to professional providers of such goods, "third stream" projects linked to engaging and serving local community needs (which must be carefully planned and monitored due to risks of mission drift and management challenges), and connecting students and learners to constituents with potential for future placement of graduates.[2]

These and related efforts to become both monetarily responsible and sustainable in the midterm to longer term are admirable, yet they are the minimum of what should be expected in the current climate. However, these measures, as necessary as they are, in many respects represent the new "new" in the contemporary global economy. These are not once-for-all fixes that will lock in the future of theological education.[3] Adding students does not always increase cash flow, as more students also escalate operational costs. Likewise, new program costs are mostly underestimated, while revenue draws from them are often overestimated. Further, while alternative delivery models are required economically, they bring with them new pedagogical challenges as they launch schools on perhaps unintended formative trajectories that may not complement our explicitly named and hoped-for outcomes. Finally, institutions of theological education can trim administrators, faculty, and staff only so much before they are ineffectual and enervated for their specific tasks. There are no shortcuts for supporting and enabling the thriving of these personal (and personnel) resources.

We can and must do all the above in some measure, but a flourishing future of theological education cannot depend only on these cost-cutting responses. Part of the challenge is that if theological institutions become only market driven, they will have been reduced to engaging the task of theological education on alien terms. The book of Revelation, for instance, admonishes its original audience about the impending judgment on the "global" Roman/Babylonian economy, one that included all "the kings of the earth, who committed fornication and lived in luxury with her [Rome], [who] will weep and wail over her when they see the smoke of her burning; they will stand far off, in fear of her torment, and say, 'Alas, alas, the great city, / Babylon, the mighty city! / For in one hour your judgment has come.' And the merchants of the earth weep and mourn for her, since no one buys their cargo anymore" (Rev. 18:9–11). The warning is that those who participate in and put their trust in the economic regimes of this world inevitably get caught up in a similar fate, so that when the system unravels, they experience market failure of an apocalyptic sort.[4] So, on the one hand, divinity has to "sell," not necessarily in the sense of being profitable according to the logic of the neoliberal market, but at least in terms of being responsible with its bills and obligations; but on the other hand, theological education cannot merely be commercialized without risking its purposes in the short run and its very soul in the long run.

Business as Mission: Connecting to Theological Vocation

There is one variable that deserves more elaboration: the digitization of higher education generally and of theological education more specifically. I noted in chapter 3 that the nature of the church is itself being affected by the electronic revolution, and that education itself is being transfigured. It is not just that educational offerings are being expanded through online modalities, although the wider accessibility such initiatives afford is cause for celebration. The present issue has more to do with the bureaucratic managerialism that digital technology enables.[5] On the one hand, digitization allows for unparalleled empirical measures of cost-effectiveness at every level of theological education, much of it helpful in identifying what is productive and sustainable; but on the other hand, the quantification of increasing domains of educational assessment risks reducing all activities to the digital realms of zeros and ones and becoming oblivious to other realities and perspectives.[6]

It can feel as if digitization is a compounding factor in the economics of theological education. The impact can be perceived from both the supply and the demand sides. With regard to supply, theological information is more readily available today than ever before. Not only do we have more theological texts than ever fully in the public domain, but theological scholarship is also being digitized variously, including in open-access formats (see also chap. 9). Anyone who is interested can read blogs and opinion pieces produced by scholars and other theologians-in-the-making, as well as watch recorded lectures by renowned professors, access archived colloquia and symposia, attend simulcasted conferences, participate in electronic theological discussion groups, and enjoy many other modalities of theological learning available online. And it is not just those who have terminal degrees from the established theological guild who are contributing to these conversations; autodidacts and others with varying levels of qualifications are also being drawn into the mix of the networked information economy. There is no shortage of theological information for digital consumption. Indeed, there is so much of it that those interested in theological learning cannot digest the available resources in a lifetime.

On the demand side, in our hyperconnected world information is becoming more and more a public good. With access expanding globally as technological infrastructure connects more and more people to the Internet, those so linked expect to find there almost anything they are looking for. Consequently, the questions are at least twofold for theological education: First, what does it mean for those who embark on such a course of study to have to engage with faculty and curriculum? And second, why would anyone undertake such a venture in the first place? While we will take up the former matter in part 3 of this book, the latter strikes at the heart of the economics of theological education: Who will be able to afford or be willing to pay for graduate-level education in theology, particularly when relevant information is more accessible than ever before in human history? Even if financial resources were not an issue, what is the wisdom of investing financially in formal education as opposed to becoming learned through means other than getting a degree? What is the cost-benefit ratio of going to x theological institution to study with y and z professors when the work of these scholars is otherwise accessible—and often for free?

Theological education is justifiable only on the basis of the gospel. Unless theological education empowers and equips students for proclamation of that good news in word and deed, it cannot warrant its existence. It cannot justify itself using nothing more than the market logic of the neoliberal economy. Doing business only as educational institutions rather than being drawn to the *basileia tou theou* sets us on a slippery slope, if not a straight path, toward bankruptcy both theological and financial. But as missional commitments shape both ecclesial identities—personal, ecclesial, and organizational—and the works of these hands, theological education so focused and directed can inspire participation in the redemptive activity of the triune God.

At a very concrete level, we might expect that a missional vision and mission for theological education translated economically might ensure explicit thinking about and engaging with the socioeconomic realities of this world. Courses like "Business as Mission" are addressing the task of missional engagement with the socioeconomic realities of our networked world[7]— especially searching for biblical models for thinking about such initiatives—and theological schools are adding courses of study and even whole programs on development, public theology, political theology, and environmental theology, all of which have economic dimensions.[8] That these developments are to be applauded should be clear. Yet they ought to be driven not only by market (and demand) factors—which will assimilate and domesticate the gospel into the current neoliberal economic world order—but also by missional allegiances. How ought the church as the dynamic body of Jesus and fellowship of his Spirit be mobilized for instantiating the *basileia tou theou* that is already here in some respects but also yet to come?

The book of Revelation's image of the new Jerusalem as being oriented around the divine—rather than imperial—economy envisions the city's illumination by the triune God. In this context, the seer notes: "The nations will walk by its light [the divine radiance and brilliance], and the kings of the earth will bring their glory into it. . . . People will bring into it the glory and the honor of the nations" (Rev. 21:24, 26). This is consistent with the apocalyptic depiction of those "from every tribe and language and people and nation" (5:9b) gathered around the throne of the Lamb. The *basileia tou theou*, namely, will be manifestly transethnic, translingual, and transnational, involving not just the many tongues but the many socioeconomic and political levels of creaturely constitution, from kings to citizens.

If on the one hand the economics of higher education press the question of why one should continue to pursue graduate levels of study in the present information economy, on the other hand economic conditions may demand both formal credentials and the relational networks that come with them. These forces may push some to seek theological education. Beyond meeting such market demands, however, theological education ought also to empower the church's participation in the redemptive work of the triune God that seeks to draw not just all peoples but also kings and their sociopolitical and economic regimes into the theo-political economy of the divine *basileia*. If the networked economy empowers the many voices for this-worldly sharing of information, then the ecclesial economy can harness these many accents for missional transformation. The latter will include, even if it cannot be reduced to, the politics and economics of this world.

Apostolic Sharing: Endowing Theological Education

What does such inclusion without reduction look like? What does it mean to say that theological education's empowerment of the church's mission involves the social, political, environmental, and economic realms and yet transcends them? The final part of this chapter examines these matters by retrieving the apostolic testimony.[9]

I find it noteworthy that the Pentecost gift of the Spirit for the eschatological ("last days") and empowered witness to Jesus had both educational and economic implications. Saint Luke described the immediate outcome as involving initiation into both the name of Jesus and the community gathered around him: "They devoted themselves to the apostles' teaching and fellowship, to the breaking of bread and the prayers. Awe came upon everyone, because many wonders and signs were being done by the apostles. All who believed were together and had all things in common; they would sell their possessions and goods and distribute the proceeds to all, as any had need" (Acts 2:42–45). As the apostolic teaching and doctrine are directed toward the *basileia tou theou*, normed as they are according to the person and instruction of Jesus himself, it might even be expected that such orientation to the coming divine rule includes rather than neglects the Jubilee ideals carried over in the messianic preaching that we have seen recorded in the Third Gospel (the prequel volume to Acts). The common sharing of all things is not a sub-sidiary expression of the *missio Dei* but part and parcel of what it means to embrace the life and message of Jesus as prefiguring the rule of God to come.

This communality, of course, is not without its constraints within the context of the Greco-Roman imperial economy. Later in the Acts account, we see that the sustainability of the Jubilee ideals is fraught, given the interconnections between the so-ciocultural and political-economic registers: sharing presumes communicative frames that can cross both ethno-linguistic and sociocultural divides, and the chasm between Palestinian-Jewish perspectives and broader Hellenist and Jewish-diaspora experi-ences was wider than could be overcome in the longer run (see Acts 6:1–2). Yet, recall that Pentecost empowerment directly manifested tangible socioeconomic consequences rather than being a one-off occurrence. Further elaboration confirms that such allocation and redistribution of resources were embedded in the apostolic witness and mission, at least in its relatively early days:

> Now the whole group of those who believed were of one heart and soul, and no one claimed private ownership of any posses-sions, but everything they owned was held in common. With great power the apostles gave their testimony to the resurrection of the Lord Jesus, and great grace was upon them all. There was not a needy person among them, for as many as owned lands or houses sold them and brought the proceeds of what was sold. They laid it at the apostles' feet, and it was distributed to each as any had need. There was a Levite, a native of Cyprus, Joseph, to whom the apostles gave the name Barnabas (which means "son of encour-agement"). He sold a field that belonged to him, then brought the money, and laid it at the apostles' feet. (4:32–37)

The many tongues of Pentecost galvanized many forms of re-sourcefulness, engaging a cross section of the messianic com-munity to create a form of alternative economic experiment that bridged socioeconomic classes for both practical and missional purposes, and so concretely bearing witness to the resurrection of Jesus.[10]

In our twenty-first-century context, the economic register is woven into the theological education endeavor even if it is not bound unquestioningly to the neoliberal commercial framework. The economic dimension must be adhered to, to sustain human life minimally, but its theological and missiological overlay in the apostolic situation invites a similar disposition: yes, theological education must be responsible at the business level, but the economic model ought to serve the missional commitment of empowering the diversity of ecclesial witnesses to the coming *basileia*. The apostolic witness indicates that those who have encountered the Spirit of Jesus were impelled to live out an economically radical way of life; so also today, experience of the living Christ can motivate new forms of solidarity, community, and sharing, even in ways that support the formation, education, and witness of the people of God.

Apostolic economics that harness the various levels of resources via the Spirit's multilingual witness can thus inspire our reconsideration of the fiscal sustainability of contemporary theological education. None of these is a new proposal, but all foreground the missional commitments that (should) undergird the *raison d'être* of theological institutions vis-à-vis our networked society. The big question is how to connect with others in the missional task so as to harness the resources necessary for our variety of missional purposes. Some ecclesial relationships ought to be nurtured in order to correlate educational endeavors with missional priorities. Also, organizational connections—with nongovernmental organizations, businesses, nonprofits, civic and community groups, social institutions, and a whole range of other types—could be made and fortified to produce mutual benefits. The key here is to identify and establish common cause with institutional and especially organizational others who may gain from theological perspectives—but only as such collaboration advances the messianic witness to the *basileia tou theou*.

Yet, perhaps most importantly and still to be tapped into more deeply, our networked information economy opens up other venues for the mission of the church, mediated through theological education, to reach and engage a wider audience. The Internet and open educational initiatives have already begun to reimagine the university in a networked world. One modality of responses is a networked scaffolding of theological information, engaging any and all interested laity at the baseline level, serving unaccredited ministerial and missional educational needs at a higher level, modulated to undergraduate theological learning at a third level, reconfigured for graduate-level learners and seminarians after that, and then mentoring doctoral formation as well. This may be a hierarchically organized distribution, but the organizational and connectional power of the Internet can facilitate as many informal and formal linkages between the levels as exist among those with interest and time so that the public good that is theological information can be as widely distributed as possible. All who are interested in theological education can move in and out of or "climb" these venues as desired, even while theological conversation will be gradually extended as people realize that the opportunities for theological learning are accessible and relevant to their needs. We will return later to clarify the programmatic and curricular aspects of such a rearrangement. The key here is that the many voices that are already resounding across electronic networks can find the relevant information and relationships needed to promote theological learning. Those at any and every level can connect down and up—or across and over—in order to engage in theological conversation, teaching and learning simultaneously in order to share in the apostolic teaching and discern its relevance for missional participation in the present political economy.

Such collaborative sharing of theological knowledge and information is not exactly what the apostolic community of "haves" and "have-nots" did in pooling and reallocating its resources, but the principle is similar. To be clear: I am not suggesting that we abandon the task of developing endowments as traditionally practiced in higher educational enterprises. In fact, beyond sharing of information, and even personnel—faculty, staff, and administrative—why not the even more radical sharing of endowments?! My point is to invite pause long enough to consider how theological institutions already variously connected and related can tap into the individual and collective resources made available through the network economy in order to endow theological learning that is directed to and driven by pursuit of the *missio Dei* and its attendant *basileia*. Theological educators will have to make many structural adjustments to live fully into the possibilities of this missional vision, which I clarify later (part 3), but drilling deeper into the educational empowerment of student hands for such missional agency next will consolidate the needed platform for that discussion.

Personal Formation

Participating in the Triune Community

The argument so far in this part of the book is that theological education needs to be locked into its fundamental rationale in order to avoid being misdirected by other important but not ultimate concerns, and that to be so focused is to press into the missiological question regarding the hands of the church working toward the coming reign of God. Our movement began through comprehension of the broadest compass of that missional orientation, the public sphere itself, including human witness and working amid and on behalf of the terrestrial environment that is slated also for the eschatological renewal of all things. It then zeroed in on an important dimension of that public space—the economic realm—especially given the pressures contemporary theological education has been under on this front. We have sought in each case to understand theologically both ecclesial beliefs and practices in the public-political and economic registers, especially in the light of the Pentecost outpouring of the Spirit in the last days foreshowing the Jubilee *basileia tou theou*.

The next step into this missional vortex of our educational institutions is to examine the interpersonal dimensions of participatory witness through which messianic discipleship engages the economic and public domains. To that end, this chapter explores how embodied, interethnic, and interculturally constituted human beings are rehabituated into the *missio Dei* in order to anticipate theological education's role in these processes. The chapter follows the Pentecost narrative (Acts 2) in exploring the character of devotional, dialogical, and ethical/communal practices through which those who are filled with the power of the Spirit bear missional witness to the ends of the earth (Acts 1:8). These interlinked dimensions of formation develop the vocational character that persists through whatever jobs or employment positions we might hold while facilitating, by the Spirit of Jesus, participation in and contribution to the just rule of the *missio Dei* in the present age.

This chapter also explicates the nexus where the public, the economic, and the personal come together. It moves from the wider ecclesial spheres of communal worship, witness, and sharing (chaps. 4–5) to the more intimate level of interactive and interpersonal relations. While the third and final part of this book will engage more explicitly *how* the curricular, pedagogical, and scholarly aspects of theological education work formationally and intellectually for missional witness in these domains, here I explore the practical shape of human hands laboring toward the *basileia tou theou*, particularly the affective, dialogical, ethical, and interrelated aspects that form learners (the *who* of theological education) for missional participation (the *why* of the enterprise).

Upon All Flesh: Affective Devotion of the Christic Body

Theological education ought to form and empower the church's witness to the divine reign. Luke's account of the Spirit's outpouring at Pentecost, intended precisely for such empowerment, provides one venue for reflecting on these formative tasks: "When the day of Pentecost had come, they were all together in one place. And suddenly from heaven there came a sound like the rush of a violent wind, and it filled the entire house where they were sitting. Divided tongues, as of fire, appeared among them, and a tongue rested on each of them. All of them were filled with the Holy Spirit and began to speak in other languages, as the Spirit gave them ability" (Acts 2:1–4). At least three considerations in this text invite comment.

First, note that the Spirit's outpouring comes upon those who are gathered together. Yes, there is a spatial togetherness—"in one place"—but this is secondary to the fact that they were gathered at the same time—on the Day of Pentecost. The physical assembly in the upper room (1:13) is not unimportant, but what those congregating were doing—"constantly devoting themselves to prayer" (1:14a)—is more relevant. Theological education surely mobilizes those collected in traditional brick-and-mortar, upper-room-type classrooms. Yet in the contemporary networked society, theological education also proceeds digitally in electronic forums linking communally disparate spaces and times (across multiple time zones certainly) for the work of teaching and learning. Both space and time matter. More important by far, however, is what is being done in the Spirit. This invitation to common prayer refers not merely to what the Anglican handbook invites us to do but also to the specifically Pauline theological exhortation to do all things as the one fellowship of the Spirit via incessant praying and thanksgiving (1 Thess. 5:17–18; Col. 3:17). Ecclesial devotion, both collectively and individually, is manifest in the praying of Christ's body. Such common prayer and worship, the apostolic experience depicts, is missional in and of itself, as the apostles' own daily devotion not only informed their doctrinal instruction but also facilitated the addition of others to the community (Acts 2:42, 47). Only the educational endeavor bathed in prayerful and liturgical worship is missiological and theological.[1]

Second, the Lukan description of the Pentecost event is rightly summed up by Peter, drawing from the prophet Joel: that the Spirit's outpouring is "upon all flesh" (Acts 2:17a; cf. Joel 2:28). Later on the universality of this outpouring, which is the chapter's main theme, will be explored, but here the focus is on the unequivocal depiction of Pentecost as a radically embodied experience.[2] There is a sense of being enveloped by the divine wind whose violent nature pervades those who are praying together so that they not only hear the Spirit's coming but also feel it. Further, even the visual appearance of tongues of fire is not removed from the participants—as if they could remain objective observers of what was happening—but that fire "rest[s] on each of them," touching down upon them as subjects encountering the divine breath. They are drawn in fully, engaged in the depths of their subjectivity, so that they are not just filled by the divine Spirit but also begin to speak to one another, as if "from [their] innermost being" (John 7:38 NASB). This pneumatological explanation from the Fourth Gospel makes clear what is narrated about Pentecost: that far from being ethereal, the coming of the divine wind is fully palpable and kinesthetic. Neither merely objectifiable nor only subjective, the Spirit's outpouring is both extensive and intensive in the fully embodied sense, touching bodies deeply in order to orient human persons affectively and devotionally toward the *basileia tou theou*. As all this constitutes the experientially kinesthetic spirituality that is part and parcel of the encounter with the divine at the heart of the contemporary networked religiosity discussed earlier (see chap. 3 above), then if theological education does not engage this embodied and affective dimension of human devotion, it cannot hope to capture the loves and desires of human lives for the divine mission. And the route to effective engagement of human hearts can come only through embodied disciplines and practices that habituate our habits toward and nurture our desires for the coming divine reign.[3]

Third, Pentecost bridges the transcendent and the immanent, the divine and the human, God's spirit and human spirits. This is about the outpouring of the *Holy* Spirit on *creaturely* spirits-bodies. Those gathered together not just in person but in common, in patient and travailing prayer, "were filled with the Holy Spirit and began to speak in other languages, as the Spirit gave them ability" (Acts 2:4). In a moment I will explore what speaking in other languages means for theological education, but for now my focus is on the agents engaged in that task.

Both teachers and learners are recipients of the divine Spirit and live into the mission of God only as Spirit-ed vessels. The divine breath initiates contact, and those touched by that wind respond and participate in the vocation of bearing devotional witness to the imminent divine rule.

Modernity and Enlightenment rationality seek to separate the historical and empirical from the teleological, and to bifurcate the material and physical from the spiritual, and then either to marginalize or dismiss entirely the latter referents as meaningless for contemporary human life. Education that is theological, however, is about redeeming these ostracized dimensions of creaturely endeavor. More precisely, Spirit-ed theological education actually seeks not just retrieval of what is banished but also a more robust historicity and materiality than modern rationalism could imagine. This is because the Pentecost outpouring fully renews animal flesh in ways that abstract cognitivism little appreciates, that is, affectively, devotionally, and purposively. Pentecostal formation—again: not that of the modern movement going by that label but of the normative Lukan vision— thus attends to our embodied physicality, but not in any reductive sense. Instead, human bodies are understood as intimately and intricately intertwined with human hearts (feelings), loves (devotion), and hopes (anticipations and purposes), and these fundamental elements are energetically harnessed by the Spirit to bear embodied witness, differentially and pluralistically, to the coming divine reign.[4]

From Every Nation under Heaven: Ethnic and Cultural Dialogue by the Spirit

Chapter 2 noted the multinational, global, and catholic nature of the church and its enterprise of theological education, and chapter 4 noted that ecclesial practices are political in part due to the transethnic and transcultural character of the people of God. Both claims derived from the Lukan observation that the Pentecost event involved those "from every nation under heaven"

(Acts 2:5). Here, however, I wish to press further into this aspect of the Pentecost narrative by delving into the glossolalic character of this multiculturality. Here again is Luke's narrative:

> Now there were devout Jews from every nation under heaven living in Jerusalem. And at this sound the crowd gathered and was bewildered, because each one heard them speaking in the native language of each. Amazed and astonished, they asked, "Are not all these who are speaking Galileans? And how is it that we hear, each of us, in our own native language? Parthians, Medes, Elamites, and residents of Mesopotamia, Judea and Cappadocia, Pontus and Asia, Phrygia and Pamphylia, Egypt and the parts of Libya belonging to Cyrene, and visitors from Rome, both Jews and proselytes, Cretans and Arabs—in our own languages we hear them speaking about God's deeds of power." (Acts 2:5-11)

Modern pentecostal and charismatic emphases historically have been on the many tongues of Pentecost, but in this context I suggest that this multilinguality invites consideration of the dialogical character of the church's participation in the *missio Dei*. Let me elaborate textually and missionally before exploring the implications for theological education.

Note that Luke reiteratively underlines that the miracle of Pentecost involves bewilderment "because each one heard them speaking in the native language of each" and amazement and astonishment since the large crowd that gathers from around the known (Mediterranean) world "hear, each of us, in our own native language." Those gathered from the ends of the earth—Luke accentuates especially the presence of Jews and proselytes from Rome—somehow comprehend in their own languages the deeds of divine power. That Luke intends his to be a sample listing of all of humanity in her vast ethnic, linguistic, and cultural diversity is clear in his insistence that representatives from "every nation under heaven" were gathered at this event. Hence, Pentecost can be comprehended, paradoxically through its dissonant linguistic glossolalia, as the supremely dialogical character of the *basileia tou theou*. The notion of *dialogue* meant here is not about people from different cultures sitting around a table chitchatting (although that is not excluded) but about the raucous cacophony of multiple tongues and languages redemptively renewed by the Spirit so that the church is constituted essentially by her ethnic, cultural, and linguistic pluri- and multivocality.

Ecclesial mission is thus carried out by these many tongues, languages, ethnicities, and cultures in and through the Spirit. Thus, Saint Paul's "to the Jew first and also to the Greek" (Rom. 1:16; 2:9–10) and "no longer Jew or Greek" (Gal. 3:28; cf. Col. 3:11) are not about eliminating the *differences* between the two but about forming a new people of God that *includes* both—and indeed, all—groups of people in their formerly alienating differentiatedness precisely by including (through the Spirit) the radical plurality of the non-Jew into the body of Christ.[5] The church is perhaps practically a "color-blind" community, then, insofar as being Greek or gentile is not automatically disqualifying for membership among the covenant people of God as perhaps some understood at the time, but it is *not* color-blind in the present historical context insofar as that context underlies and perpetuates the colonial ideology of white normativity. More pointedly, the many tongues of Pentecost call attention to the profound multilingual discursivity of the fellowship of the Spirit so that its ecumenical catholicity is constituted by multiracial, interethnic, and cross-cultural dialogue understood as theological and educational values rather than as the political dominance of any single majority group.[6] Missional participation in the Spirit's renewing and redemptive work therefore unfolds dialogically through many languages. Put differently, missional witness is carried out not uni-directionally but from everywhere to everywhere.[7] Even in the Acts narrative, missional discipleship proceeds not only from Jerusalem to Rome but also from Rome (at the putative ends of the earth) to Jerusalem (the center of the world from the apostolic perspective): from the Jews and proselytes who were from Rome and yet at the Pentecost event, where they proclaimed the wondrous works of God to the world gathered on the streets of this central Jewish city (Acts 2:10–11).

What does this dialogical inter-, multi-, and transculturality mean for theological education? I propose what Samuel Calian calls the "multiculturalization" of theological education: a thoroughly multiethnic and multicultural set of dialogical practices—involving sympathetic listening as much as conversational discussion, active argument as much as forging of agreement, exploratory imagination as much as clarifying positions—that is constitutive of and central to deepening the church's missional catholicity.[8] Theological education as we now know it remains deeply rooted in Western traditions and languages. The Pentecost soundscape does not eliminate this Western witness but abolishes its hegemony and does so by recognizing at least two distinct dynamics, one internal to the so-called West and the other considering the current ferment in world Christianity.

First, the Pentecost narrative insists that the known world is constituted by difference and plurality, and this requires acknowledgment that the so-called West speaks not in one but in many voices. There is an internal ethnic and cultural diversity to any collective of people, and this applies not less to the West than to the "rest" (the East or the South, etc., to which I return momentarily). More importantly, there are marginal voices also amid the Western tradition. Just as Cretans and Arabs were noted as present at Jerusalem on the Day of Pentecost but yet subordinated to Romans and Jews in the apostolic imagination—we know, for instance, that Cretans were particularly stereotyped as "always liars, vicious brutes, lazy gluttons" (Titus 1:12b)[9]—so also are there minority reports galore in the Western theological tradition, whether monastic renewal movements (at the frontiers of Roman centrism), the Radical Reformation (on the edges of German Protestantism), or Wesleyan-Holiness Pentecostalism (across the American frontier and overlooking the Pacific Rim), for example. Theological education ought to retrieve and attend to these marginal voices as part of its dialogical exercise.

Second, there is no one leading voice or principal language in the transnational Pentecost event that spanned the known world from Jerusalem to Rome and everywhere and everyone in between. Theological education thus ought to listen more intently to the voices not just of the so-called non-Western traditions—which categorization still privileges the West—but of Eastern churches and the many others across the global ecumenical Christian movement. Here, of course, I am referring to Orthodox communions but also to the historical and contemporary churches dispersed amid the Asian frontier, throughout sub-Saharan Africa, across the Latin Americas, and among indigenous (including oceanic) peoples of the world, each region and categorization of which are also internally diverse and plural rather than reducible to a single register. Theological education must undergo a decentering of Western normativity, especially the decolonizing of Eurocentrism that is enshrined both in the modern ecclesial project and in the historic higher educational enterprise.[10] This is not to dismiss Western contributions but to reconsider Western perspectives amid the many ethnic-cultural tones of the church ecumenical, both historical and contemporary. Theological education thus is or ought to be utterly dialogical, emerging out of the hybridizing interactivity of the church catholic and her faithful participation in missional practice that heralds the coming reign of God amid the glocal cosmopolis.

Even upon the Slaves: Ethical Justice for Basileia Democracy

So far this chapter has considered the devotional and dialogical practices that launch members of the fellowship of the Spirit on the missional life. In these last paragraphs of this second part of the book, I turn to the ethical character of these practices, tracking especially the normative trajectory of interpersonal participation in the *missio Dei*. To that end, I continue with the Pentecost narrative, turning now to Luke's summary of Peter's explanation of the Pentecost event, drawing from the prophet Joel:

In the last days it will be, God declares,
that I will pour out my Spirit upon all flesh,
    and your sons and your daughters shall prophesy,
and your young men shall see visions,
    and your old men shall dream dreams.
Even upon my slaves, both men and women,
    in those days I will pour out my Spirit;
        and they shall prophesy.
And I will show portents in the heaven above
    and signs on the earth below,
        blood, and fire, and smoky mist.
The sun shall be turned to darkness
    and the moon to blood,
        before the coming of the Lord's great and
            glorious day.
Then everyone who calls on the name of the Lord shall
    be saved. (Acts 2:17–21; cf. Joel 2:28–31)

The primary message summing up the achievement of Pentecost, that "everyone who calls on the name of the Lord shall be saved," is consistent with the Lukan portrayal regarding the universal character of the Spirit poured out "upon all flesh." However, the telos of the divine reign also involves the making of an egalitarian, democratic, and justly ordered community—all core elements of missional witness and theological education.

For us in the third decade of the third millennium and onward, it is easy to overlook the radical nature of the Pentecost empowerment of *both* sons *and* daughters *equally*, a message that is at the heart of egalitarian readings of the New Testament. Women gained suffrage in the Western world only about a century ago. For most of human history, certainly at the time of Joel's prophecy and even amid the late first-century Pax Romana when Luke wrote, it would have been completely unexpected to say (as Paul also did: e.g., Gal. 3:28) that being female did not disqualify one from participation in the Spirit's renewing work but actually was part and parcel of God's plan for enabling witness heralding the divine rule. The Lukan understanding of women as participating equally in the prophetic practice of bearing witness to the reign of God itself should not be subordinated as of secondary import in considering afresh male and female relations. At the least, male authoritarianism is undercut by the Pentecost outpouring. If patriarchal domination is undermined, then women are equal disciples rather than second-class citizens in the *basileia tou theou*. Theological education needs to wrestle with this egalitarian pronouncement and actively promote its ecclesial and missional embodiment.

The Pentecost account also promotes a form of democratic empowerment, at least in equalizing the voices and perspectives of young and old. In gerontocratic societies like those of the ancient Mediterranean world, older members of the community were privileged for their experiential and political wisdom. The New Testament does not minimize the honor due to parents and other elders, but the renewing work of the Spirit also does not render subservient the visions of youth to the dreams of the elderly. The point is not to displace the latter's dreams with the former's visions, but no longer to presume priority for the older generation's preferences and assumptions. What are the implications for relationships between junior faculty and senior professors, or between learners (students) and instructors (tenured too), for instance? Missional witness proceeds in multiple directions, and theological education should nurture these democratic intuitions, sensibilities, and commitments.

Last but not least, the egalitarian and democratic character of the Pentecost Spirit is intrinsic to the divine rule's righting of injustices that polarize societies between the haves and the have-nots. In the ancient world, as in today's network society, the chasm between the socioeconomically and politically privileged and those on the underside of history remains wide. The radical promise of Pentecost is that even the "slaves"—*doulos* in the Greek—are emancipated for missional participation. The Spirit's outpouring neither bypasses nor is withheld from those relegated by the socioeconomic powers-that-be to the dregs of society. In fact, the messianic arrival was precisely for their sake, as Luke explicitly documents in his prequel volume:

> "The Spirit of the Lord is upon me,
>   because he has anointed me
>   to bring good news to the poor.
> He has sent me to proclaim release to the captives
>   and recovery of sight to the blind,
>   to let the oppressed go free." (Luke 4:18)

Not surprisingly, then, as the early disciples embarked on their missional journey in the power of the Spirit of Jesus their Lord, the results were such that they became known as those who had "been turning the world upside down" (Acts 17:6). Wrongs were being righted; the marginalized were being empowered; the lowly were being lifted up. Pentecost enables witness to the coming divine rule by introducing new imaginative possibilities and endowing concomitant practices for all: male and female, older and younger, the haves and the have-nots. The last come not only to "have" as a result of apostolic sharing; they also come to participate in the missional task, anticipating the *basileia tou theou*.

This world consists of inequalities of many and all kinds. The gospel arrives into this situation in order to name another possible way of being in the world, and the gift of the Spirit enables the people of God to begin to live out that possibility, at least in part, while waiting, not passively but in missional hope and activity, for the full establishment of the divine rule that is on its way. Such missional witness and practices, we have seen in this chapter, are born out of lives and relationships transformed by an encounter with the resurrected Christ, knitted together in and through the fellowship of his Spirit, so that individually and collectively devotional, dialogical, and ethical practices might be carried out amid a world that is sometimes watching and reacting but otherwise often oblivious to the presence and activity of God's rule. Authentic witness enabled by the Pentecost Spirit will have wider socioeconomic (chap. 5) and sociopolitical (chap. 4) effects and implications. This is how theological learners are vocationally formed to leave a legacy that persists beyond their jobs and even their lives on this side of the eschaton.[11]

So far, then, I have considered the *who* of theological education—the church in its global, multicultural, and networked permutations in the present epoch—and its *why*: the church's missional practices of heralding/proclaiming the rule of God in the public square, sharing its resources in a world of economic scarcity, and forming hearts and lives devotionally, dialogically, and ethically. These are the fundamental ecclesiological and missiological dimensions of the church's educational imperative. No doubt the questions have doubled since the end of the first part of this book, but the answers I suggest are less practical resolutions than they are means to empower the theological—specifically, *pneumatological*—imagination to grapple with these dynamic and fluid realities. So, if the question is *how* theological education can hope to accomplish its tasks of empowering rapidly changing forms of the church in its missional witness, the answer has to be ecclesiological, missiological, and pneumatological: by living as the church and participating in the *missio Dei* by the power of the Holy Spirit. The third and final part of this book makes explicit the curricular, pedagogical, and scholarly commendations whose ecclesial, missional, and pneumatic outlines have already emerged in the foregoing discussions.

3

Academy in Glocal Contexts

The Mind and Task of Theological Exploration

Theological Curriculum

Teaching by the Spirit of Truth

We have arrived, having started from the heart of theological education (the church) and having traversed the hands of theological education (mission in and to the world), at the so-called head of theological education: the academy. Understood by such a pathway, theological education is not merely cognitive but also holistic in connecting the intellectual with the affective and the practical. Our task in this third and final part of this book, then, is to reconceive the work of theological education (the *how*) as involving both the ecclesial/ecclesiological (the *who*) and missional/missiological (the *why*) dimensions.

How then does theological education engage the *who* toward and for the *why?* The three chapters of this third part of the book turn to those aspects often prominent in discussions of theological education: its curricular, pedagogical, and scholarly components. Hence, we discuss the accumulated knowledge that is to be critically retrieved by the next generation, the process or modes of such reception and reappropriation, and the quest for new knowledge or its application and related tasks. Here I assume that teaching and research are fundamentally entwined moments and activities of the vocation of theological education.

Here, as throughout this book, my focus is on the work of the Spirit. What inspires me are the scriptural references to the interdependence of the Spirit of truth (e.g., John 17:17; 15:26; 16:13; 1 John 4:6), the Spirit of wisdom (e.g., Deut. 34:9; Isa. 11:2; Eph. 1:17), and the spiritual worship that renews the mind (Rom. 12:1–2). I thus propose that a spirited program of theological study appropriate to the present cosmopolitical network should be informed by dynamic ecclesial realities, orienting missional commitments, and innovative interdisciplinary approaches. Consequently, I organize our curricular discussion into these three domains but engage each less in terms of content and more in terms of how they provide hermeneutical and methodological routes for theological study. My focus in the following is thereby less on a question like, *What is the church?*—which we traversed in part 1 above—and more on the hermeneutical question, *How does being the pluriform church open up a path of theological inquiry?* My emphasis is less on *What is mission?*—which we navigated in the preceding part—and more on the methodological query, *How does a missiological imagination prompt certain ways of asking and seeking understanding of the important theological questions of our time?* These ecclesiological and missiological ventures, as I argued above, are already interdisciplinary in the present landscape. Hence, I take them in order, not because they are disparate but to ensure adequate treatment of our distinctive approach to re-visioning the theological curriculum for our contemporary period.

From the Laity to the Professoriate: An Ecclesial Hermeneutic

What does it mean for theological education to be structured ecclesially? What does the theological curriculum look like when ecclesially organized? How do we think not just about the church but with and as the church? And what difference does this make for theological education?

While the question of the church is in some respects a problem to be resolved, the church is also a hermeneutical lens through which we can begin to sort out the important theological issues and questions of the networked era. About a quarter of a century ago, missionary theologian Lesslie Newbigin proposed viewing the congregation as a "hermeneutic of the gospel," by which he meant that local congregations provide windows into the shape of the Christian message.[1] I build off his insight to explore the shape of the theological curriculum in our post-Christendom and networked era, but expand his congregational focus to the broader ecclesiological question.

Our hermeneutical starting point could be the form and character of the evolving church in the present and the viewpoints this presents for theological inquiry. Scripturally, for instance, how does the contemporary variegated shape of the church provide new lenses through which to reconsider what it means to be the body of Christ (in the New Testament) and the people of God (in the Hebrew Bible) and for understanding the nature of divine covenants and election? How might experiences of charismatic renewal inform our understanding of the institutional and hierarchical church in relationship not just to its presumed margins but also to its increasingly networked reality? How can previously settled questions about who and what we are as the church, now troubled by contemporary developments, become springboards for revisiting Scripture and tradition as we reconstruct what it means to be the people of God in today's flat world? It is not that the traditional curriculum has to be dismantled but that its culturally and historically contingent character, including especially its colonial and racialized form bequeathed from the early modern period, ought to be interrogated, and that whatever survives ought to be carried forward critically. That we have done theological education in this or that way for the last two hundred years or more is not sufficient reason for continuing the same.

Today's theological curriculum should enable learners to ask questions both about their collective (i.e., ecclesial) and individual (personal) identities, since *who we are* (and what we do) is connected to *who I am* (and what I do), and vice versa. Theological education should thus enable learners to connect the ecclesial and the existential/vocational spheres. Scriptural interpretation and historical retrieval, in this scheme, are related to contemporary anxieties about who we are and of what communities of belonging we are a part. Traditionally, theological education has sought to form clergy or ministers, but in the networked society, we realize that such persons are not mere individuals but are communally and discursively shaped. In fact, the Reformation motto of the priesthood of all believers persists with a new twist in a connected twenty-first century since each voice is potentially amplifiable electronically. The question is how to discern the ecclesial shape of our communal lives if the digital world blurs the boundaries of the church's nestedness within other social forms and realities. What does it look like to be a minister today when the lines between clergy and laity are less clear than they were in the Christendom era? Or, for institutions of theological education that have had or wish to include doctoral programs of study: What does it look like to exercise professional or scholarly leadership when this builds bridges from the church to the professions in one direction (the professional doctorate) or to the academy in the other direction (the PhD in relevant fields)? Hence, although our reformulated theological curriculum will continue to include ministerial and scholarly formation, in this networked era we must ask difficult questions about what ministry (and mission) and scholarship look like so that our courses of study can be adjusted accordingly.

Theological education today ought to be attentive to the question of personal formation that necessarily involves the collective or communal domain. That communal domain is best understood through the lens of ecclesiology. Here we are not only trying to identify the who or what of the church; we are also attempting to discern what the shape and form of the church is and ought to be, and, by extension, what is or ought to be the shape and form of our own lives and vocations in a changing world. All our theological resources must be brought to bear on this task: scriptural interpretation, historical reappropriation, and expansive theological imagination. Our self-understanding is entwined with our realization that we are part of an environmentally rooted and covenantal community whose present identity and ultimate purposes are always open for reformulation as we respond to and interact with the call of the *basileia tou theou*.

As the Pentecost account shows that the founding of the church is interrelated with the outpouring of the Spirit, so too the ecclesiological and the pneumatological are two sides of one theological coin. To discern the church is to discern the Spirit that inspires confession of the Lord of the church; to hear the church is to hear the Spirit who speaks what the Lord of the church says; to build the church is to follow the Spirit that enables participation in the body of Christ. Thus, the pneumatological and the ecclesiological are both points of entry into theology proper: the doctrine of God revealed in Jesus Christ by the Holy Spirit.

The church is both a hermeneutic of the gospel (Newbigin) and a methodological guideline for theological inquiry. The traditional theological curriculum can be advanced, now ecclesially directed and pneumatically assisted. We are not talking about courses on the Holy Spirit but about the entirety of the theological curriculum refracted through both Easter and Pentecost. The vocational possibilities of theological education can and should be adapted for a networked society, but these will be embedded in ecclesiological questions and pneumatological concerns. Our programs of study should facilitate student inquiry connecting personal identity with ecclesiological and pneumatological perspectives.

Church-Mission-World:
A Missional Approach to Theological Inquiry

Clearly, Newbigin's congregational hermeneutic was missiologically embedded. A viable theological curriculum for the present networked age must likewise deploy both ecclesial and missional approaches in its theological inquiry. What does it mean for theological education to be structured not just ecclesially but also practically and missionally? What does the theological curriculum look like when missionally organized? How do we think not just about the church's mission but with such ministry and witness? And what difference does this make for theological education?

These questions ask how we understand ourselves, enabling a kind of self-care or soul care, while this next segment considers our purposes, orienting ourselves beyond us. These are two essential considerations in a connected and relational world. Now I turn to explore how a missional course of study opens up the meeting of church and world in all its dynamic and shifting complexity. Questions about mission and witness thus uncover that the apostolic sending into the world redraws the lines of "inside" and "outside," just as incarnation situates the Word in creational history and Pentecost breathes the divine breath into creaturely flesh.

A missional approach to theological education therefore reorients the dominant theological curriculum and forces us to reconsider education from without, as it were. Whereas the currently prevailing theological curriculum locates the practice of ministry as the application of what was discovered in biblical exegesis, historical understanding, and theological study, a missional approach to education interrogates this ministerial moment from within and insists that education is not just about developing certain skills to be applied in the practice of ministry. Rather, the practice of ministry in new and previously unexplored contexts should return us to the rest of the curriculum with fresh hermeneutical and methodological considerations. That is, the study of Scripture should be read missiologically in light of new relationships and challenges;[2] Christian history and its sophisticated historiographic methods now also become mission history, and vice versa, in new settings and environments;[3] and the entirety of the theological loci—both dogmatics and systematics, including the speculative and constructive moments of the theological task— ought also to be practically and missionally reconsidered in light of advances of society and knowledge.[4] Understood like this, practical Christian discipleship and mission are no longer incidental add-ons to the center of theological education; rather, the arenas of practical theology and mission studies become theological methodologies and modes of curricular organization and inquest: *praxis and mission become the dual lenses through which we embark on theological inquiry and by which we reimagine theological study and learning.* As with our proposed ecclesial hermeneutic (above), this does not necessarily involve a complete replacement of the present curriculum by a new (practical or missional) program; but it does provide new approaches, prompt new concerns, and bring new perspectives to familiar scriptural, historical, and theological terrain from the margins of where Christian witness resounds regarding the coming divine reign.

And it is these new contexts where church meets world that generate fresh questions. The so-called hermeneutical spiral means that ministry and mission are intrinsic to the task of theological inquiry since they are the contextual sites through which biblical, historical, and theological work is applied, communicated, and tested.[5] The latter confronts us with questions regarding the relevance and significance of our theological course of study. What Scripture meant then is interrelated with what Scripture means for us now and today. It is not that the former is reducible to the latter, but that apart from the latter, the study of Scripture ceases to be theologically life giving in the fullest sense for the present ecclesial and missional community. What happened then (in history) is interwoven with what happens now (in the present); again, not that the former becomes whatever the latter dictates, but that contemporary realities across world Christianity motivate inquiry into our predecessors' realities. What has been dogmatically pronounced (in the West, particularly) is interlinked with what is theologically constructed (today in vastly different places and times), since each new cultural and linguistic context retrieves and reappropriates the complex heritage of the past in different ways. Thus, as Christian life unfolds in a global and networked world, ministerial and missional contexts catalyze fresh scriptural, historical, and theological questions.

This is not to dismiss altogether the practical theological and missiological curricula currently on offer, but to reset their trajectory, now understood more clearly than ever before as fundamentally interconnected with contexts of mission and ministry around the world. As we have already seen (in part 2 above), ministry and mission no longer proceed from presumptions of the church structured by Christendom, nor from the Euro-American West to the so-called "rest," nor from knowledge mediated through the Western Enlightenment, etc. In a post-Christendom, postcolonial, and postfoundationalist networked world, practical theology and missiology cannot but be thoroughly relational, dialogical, multicultural, and multidirectional. Practical theological topics—from liturgical studies to counseling, from pastoral ministry to leadership, from congregational studies to cultural ethnography, and so on—therefore need to be reimagined from being merely incubators of practical skills to being central to the theory-praxis feedback loop. Similarly, missiological programs and courses—from mission theory and history to church planting, from world Christianity to the study of Islam or South and East Asian cultures and religions, from cultural anthropology to urban and development studies, and so on—also need to be re-visioned from being objects of study to being subjects inviting participatory and dialogical inquiry.

Theological education will need to be committed to the task of pastoral care and ministry, and to church planting and evangelism—major themes and courses in the classical curriculum—but it cannot be done in exactly the same way as it was in the Christendom context. Westerners will need to be globally informed and not just translate—export!—the West to "the rest," even as those from the Global South will increasingly study in their own regions of the world rather than coming to the West to be inculturated into Eurocentric academic norms. Going forward, theological institutions around the world will need to collaborate more than ever in order both to avoid new forms of colonial domination and to undertake appropriate measures to decolonize the academy so that it reflects more and more the reality of the transnational people of God constituted by those from many nations, cultures, and languages.

As the Pentecost account shows, the church's witness is launched with the outpouring of the Spirit, and thus the missiological and the pneumatological are intimately interrelated. To discern the *missio Dei* is to discern the divine breath that enables confession of the one who himself embodied the ministry and mission of God; to participate in ministry and mission is to be carried by the Spirit, who speaks in the economy of the Word; to persevere ministerially and missionally is to follow the Spirit that herself takes up residence in us so that we can become guests of others and invite them to the grand banquet arranged by the host of creation. And to ask the missiological-pneumatological question is also to broach the eschatological horizon: witness to the *basileia tou theou* in the power of the one who makes present that which is both to come and on its way. Thus, the pneumatological, missiological, and eschatological are triadically interconnected points of entry into theology proper: the coming God revealed in Jesus Christ by the Holy Spirit.

Ecclesial practice and mission are both a hermeneutic of the gospel and a methodological guideline for theological inquiry. They are therefore also a guide for theological education as a whole. This is not just to emphasize programs and classes in missiology. Rather, it is a call to bring forward the entirety of the historic theological curriculum in ways that are missionally funded, pneumatically charted, and eschatologically normed. Thus, our ecclesiological and missiological curricula—by which we mean not only content but also hermeneutical and methodological approaches—are developed in a fluid and dynamic manner, guided by the ongoing discernment of what the Spirit is doing through the church in the world, even while being willing to pronounce both evangelical (gospel) encouragement and prophetic protest in accordance with the coming divine rule. The vocational horizons of theological education, which is the divine reign as revealed in Jesus and anticipated in the here and now by the work of his Spirit, can and should be heralded amidst a networked society. New courses and programs of theological study should facilitate student inquiry to connect personal vocation and formation with practical/missiological realities, pneumatological/ charismatic dynamics, and eschatological aspirations.

Many Languages, Multiple Disciplinary Connections: A Spirit-ed Theological Program

I have so far proposed that ecclesiological and missiological concerns and perspectives ought to be central to theological programs of study for a networked era. Precisely since both focus on questions of identity and practice (Who are those taking up theological education? And why do they do it?), they not only reconfigure the prevalent theological curriculum from the margins where the church meets society and the world, but they also work at their highest levels when carried out in an interdisciplinary manner. Both have historically drawn from and interacted with the human sciences, in particular with anthropological and ethnographic methods.[6] Within the field of practical theology, interdisciplinarity has been a gradual but now surely quite central endeavor. Missiology, however, in particular its "modern" version from the last half century, has long been an interdisciplinary field of inquiry, especially in its quest to comprehend human sociocultural diversity.

Such developments on the practical theological and missiological fronts parallel the growing interdisciplinarity of theological inquiry in the last generation. Here I am referring to the dialogue between theology and the natural sciences,[7] and to the growing interactions with emerging conversations in the humanities, from religious and cultural studies to literature to film and media studies. These forays can be seen as natural extensions of the perennial dialogue in the Western tradition between theology and philosophy even as this dialogue now begs for intercultural analysis (in a globally interconnected world) and comparative assessment (with other wisdom traditions around the world, both the so-called world religions and more local and indigenous traditions). And our present networked world means that our looking back historically proceeds hand in hand with our looking around at contemporary dynamics in the political, economic, and social arenas. Thus it is important that theology engage with the political, economic, and sociological sciences.

Such interdisciplinarity needs to be both curricular and methodological/programmatic. The former is needed since adept deployment within the latter requires some sort of fluency, if not mastery, of these discursive fields of inquiry. If maturity in the theological sphere is not attained except through a postgraduate program involving up to a decade of concentrated study, this is consistent with similar accomplishments in other disciplines. I have long characterized intellectual formation as parallel to cross-cultural formation:[8] both involve sustained and extensive processes of immersion into alien worlds of discursive practice in which new traditions are learned, other linguistic and symbolic codes are internalized, and additional communicative and practical repertoires are developed to levels that enable insiders of that discipline or scholarly field to confer recognition that those former aliens (outsiders) have passed successfully through some sort of certificatory exercise (course of study or cultural-religious initiation). The adept is the one who understands the content of a discipline or the *what* of any cultural form of practical inquiry and also is able to think and work subjectively and methodologically with the newly available (disciplinary or cultural) tools.

If Pentecost sustains and lifts up each in his or her own language, then the coming divine reign preserves and enhances rather than marginalizes or eliminates the diversity of cultures and peoples of the world. By extension, the outpouring of the Spirit also involves the empowering of the many disciplines, each understood as a set of discursive practices developed and refined over time that enables a dynamic community of inquiry in their inhabitation and exploration of the world. The Spirit assuredly mediates between church and world (practically and missionally),[9] but also among the discursive media (cultural and disciplinary) that facilitate our common quests for understanding. So, whereas during the colonial enterprise the renewal of the Spirit could be understood as a gifting of glossolalia that documented, preserved, and translated the languages of the many tribes and peoples of the world (which is one way to consider Lamin Sanneh's thesis about the Protestant missionary translation of Scripture),[10] in contemporary theological education such renewal can be understood also as a kind of multidiscursivity that enables the cross-fertilization of disciplinary and methodological tools across the academy for the sake of gaining knowledge and growing in truthful understanding of ourselves and our world.

Concretely, interdisciplinarity in theological education can take many forms. In its most robust form, theological or divinity schools situated within universities will have conversational partners across the hall, in a neighboring school or department, and the interdisciplinary dialogue will emerge organically. Alternatively, stand-alone seminaries or similar types of institutions of theological education can nevertheless encourage and cultivate other disciplinary perspectives in theological study, learning, and scholarship via involvement of tutors, or via cross-registration in courses available in consortia of affiliated institutions offering more diverse curricula. Last but not least, theological programs can select from their base of prospects learners with training and background in nontheological disciplines to begin with and encourage retrieval of these prior fields of study in their theological program.

In the information age, it is a truism that higher education forms lifelong learners and that the programmatic certification of a degree is less about having mastered a particular content set that is practically outdated shortly thereafter than it is about demonstrating the capacity to ask new questions and develop appropriate ways to seek after and pursue resolution. The goal here is not to resist the so-called credentialization of higher education but to take the opportunity to consider how we embrace or might embrace this task and what our certificates and credentials mean vis-à-vis our learners and their vocations in the public square. Our Spirit-ed approach seeks to provide a specifically theological warrant for lifelong learning: learners who live in the Spirit are renewed by the Spirit day by day, and this includes renewal within the intellectual realm. Theological education initiates learners into a lifelong course of Spirit-ed study, in part through introducing them into an interdisciplinary matrix, but especially by nurturing the cultivation of a diverse set of methodological tools through which they learn to pursue whatever (new) questions arise along life's networked way. At its best, theological education connects learners with other relational networks—ecclesial and missional partners or scholarly and disciplinary guilds—that make available resources for the journey of transformational and missional learning across the life span.

If interdisciplinarity is standard in higher education, we are not merely attempting to baptize it in theological terms for programs of study in divinity. This is because our pneumatological sensibilities include axiological commitments that question and even counter the operationalization of such interdisciplinarity, especially in secular academia. If the modern university comprehends disciplinary knowledge to be guided by Enlightenment values of objectivity that prioritize the discovery of truth apart from subjective biases, our Pentecost perspective is guided and normed by the revelation of God in Christ through the Spirit's ushering in of the divine rule and reign. This means that the truth toward which theological inquiry aims, which is believed also to be enabled by the Spirit of truth (see John 14:17; 15:26; 16:13), attempts to comprehend the truthful interconnected nature of all things in Christ.[11] Yet this means neither that Christian theological inquiry is incapable of engaging with other (faith) perspectives in the common quest for truth nor that such a position is presumptive—that those working in the theological disciplines would be presumed to "lord it over" other disciplinary and scholarly endeavors in the public square. The medieval period may have understood theology as the so-called queen of the sciences, but in today's climate, such stances of faith can be held only provisionally and dialogically, if at all. This means that Christian teaching is committed to the tension of an interdisciplinary and interconnected mutuality that is genuinely reciprocal and still serves to empower the church in its task of bearing humble witness to the redemptive work of the gospel in a networked (and multireligious) world.[12]

The preceding is an initial foray into the present and future theological curriculum. I proposed neither that the full scope of theological study in its classical format be gutted nor that our focus be only on a narrow curricular space. Instead, I have attempted to follow through from the discussion so far that has queried the *who* of contemporary theological education and its *what* (its purposes), and from that perspective have wondered how ecclesiology and missiology might function in the present informational and interdisciplinary matrix as hermeneutical and methodological vehicles for theological inquiry as a whole. Such a triadic hermeneutic and theological method encourages dialogical and interdisciplinary retrieval of historical resources while being attentive to dynamic intercultural realities and challenges. Ecclesiology, missiology, and interdisciplinarity thereby turn from subject areas into portals of inquiry that have the capacity to sustain learning during divinity school or seminary and also after graduation—not because they are all-encompassing but because they map onto the nexus of important questions and perspectives—the many tongues—of identity and vocation swirling in our post-Enlightenment, postcolonial, and post-Christendom world.

Theological Pedagogy

Learning in the Spirit of Wisdom

In the preceding chapter I attempted to rehabilitate the theological curriculum by observing how Pentecost perspectives offer insights into the hermeneutical and methodological engines that drive *what* we study. Now I seek a similar objective: to revitalize theological pedagogy by considering how Pentecost considerations invite reconfiguration of *how* we teach and learn. I suggest a multimodal pedagogy, one that is intrinsic to the church's networked catholicity, that is empowered by our multisensorial and multimediated connectivist technology, and that is oriented performatively and practically toward missional participation to the ends of the earth. Whereas the previous chapter focused on *what* empowers learning, here we elaborate on the *how* of such inspired learning, how knowledge is democratized so that as many learners as possible can participate in the intellectual life. As there, so here I do not assume the replacement of the ways in which we have previously taught and learned. I assume that we will need both continuity with the best practices of the past and pedagogical innovativeness that responds to and is carried by the dynamics of a new global millennium.

This part of the book suggests how theological education can be effectively accommodating to and critically engaging of the challenges and opportunities of the present networked environment.[1] The most important clue for this lies in how discussion of the theological curriculum turned from content to method (hermeneutics, theological method, and interdisciplinary modes of inquiry, more specifically). It is not that content is not important, but that in the information age how one continues to learn is just as important, given the exponential expansion of knowledge over time. Similarly, it is not only that we teach, mentor, and engage learners effectively (the focus of pedagogical studies), but that we model the connection between teaching and learning *so that we pass on wisdom*. Such wisdom is a dynamic set of ingrained habits and skills of and for discernment—what Orthodox and Wesleyan traditions call heart knowing—that can continue to inspire intellectual conversation and grow character long after the formal program of study is concluded.[2] What we are teaching is thus not only theological content but also a charismatic disposition toward learning and being receptive to what can be learned by and through the Spirit in any new situation. These pedagogical instincts and sensibilities that can be imbibed by students so that they are transformed into lifelong learners and also teachers of others are, as well, central to the activity of research and scholarship taken up in the final chapter of this book.

Languages of the Spirit: Constructivist and Dialogical Learning

Theories of contemporary teaching and learning that are attentive to our networked environment are pedagogically constructivist.[3] Such constructivism presumes that the pervasiveness of the Internet provides the basic framework for gathering information, and this is the case both for exclusively online programs of study and for traditional residential classrooms that now almost always include a digital dimension. This framework signals the end of the lecture (the professor as talking head), which is central to modernist higher education, and heralds the transformation of teachers and students into mutual learners, at least at the graduate level. The constructivism that is presumed here works with a critical realist ontology that presumes that reality exists apart from knowers, but also that knowledge of reality always includes the subject's perspective.[4] Digital learning, in a nutshell, fundamentally assumes learner agency, and our networked world opens up learner connections and constructions in at least five directions.

First, theological pedagogies will need to transition from being Eurocentric to being multi- and cross-cultural. Just as the theological curriculum needs to be decolonized, so does theological instruction need to unfold via a diversity of cultural and linguistic media. Ethnocentrism, ultranationalism, and especially nationalistic exceptionalism will need to be tempered by both the diversity internal to these categorical matrices and the pluralism of our dynamically networked world. This is not to dismiss completely Western (Euro-American) traditions and sources but to resituate their reception within a multicultural, multireligious, and global context. The fact that seminarians and divinity learners in online programs now are transnationally located and transculturally informed means that the ongoing theological conversation will inevitably extend in this direction. My claim is that we should identify and think through the theological warrants for such pedagogical reimagination—exactly what is being attempted in this book—rather than being driven only by demographic pressures.

Second, precisely because theological education is now a global undertaking, we cannot presume the dominance of Western philosophies and worldviews in the background of our conversations. Instead, a majority of theological learners will be thinking out of religious and wisdom traditions from around the world. Hence, theological education ought to facilitate interreligious and comparative philosophical dialogue as well. Such conversations should be built into the curriculum in the formal sense of enabling explicit interaction between people of various faiths and wisdom traditions, essential as such is for the future of human relations in a fragile and often violent world. They should be designed to facilitate comprehension of how the lines between religion and culture, or between religion and philosophy, are a lot more intertwined elsewhere in the world than they are in the modern West. On the one hand, theological pedagogies ought to facilitate dialogue between people of different religious and wisdom communities. On the other hand, theological learning ought also to enable attention to the internal dialogue that happens when we encounter others and realize that part of what they represent exists in our own lives in some respect; this is the *intra*religious and *intra*philosophical dialogue by people of faith.[5] Theological wisdom emerges when the interreligious dialogue and the intrareligious dialogue meet in a world of religious and philosophical dynamism, hybridity, and cross-fertilization.[6]

Third, theological pedagogy in the present era will accelerate interdisciplinary dialogue. Academic silos are no longer defensible in a global, interconnected, and constructivist world. Learners increasingly arrive at theological education shaped initially in their undergraduate studies in another discipline, and our theological courses of study ought to encourage and insist upon disciplinary integration rather than a conversion to theology in the classical manner that leaves behind these former discursive frames. Theological discourse that knows only itself not only will be irrelevant[7] but also could be said to be ignorant of theology precisely in not realizing its situatedness within the many regimes and disciplines of knowledge. If all truth is God's truth, then there is no reason for theology to recoil from substantive dialogue with the disciplines and sciences with the methodological and exploratory expertise relevant to whatever is being inquired about. This is less about theology dominating the conversation (as one model of what the medieval period meant by the notion of *theology as the queen of the sciences*) than about a genuine reciprocity of mutual discovery.

Fourth, the Internet connects people to mutual interest groups, socially, politically, economically, culturally, and otherwise. There is no reason why theological education cannot engage whatever expertise is relevant to topics of theological inquiry and study. Shared human problems, injustices, and environmental crises invite collaborative engagement for the common good across disciplines and across communities, cultures, nations, and organizations. Our networked world allows for such connective and constructive dialogue in an unparalleled manner. Experienced theological educators will create pedagogical environments that welcome learners who bring their existing networks with them into their courses of study even as they will deploy pedagogical practices that will introduce learners to new ecclesial and related resources and relationships. Theological learners, thus, are not just blank slates to be informed but nodes of connectedness that can enhance the conversation within theological classrooms and learning spaces.

Last but not least, the agency of each learner means that theological education provides a forum and venue for the emergence of each person's own voice. Such witness is part of the process of naming one's experience and then narrating one's identity in all of its contested, dynamic, and hybrid character. This testimonial empowerment is central to theological education since it enables a fresh (perhaps for the first time) accounting of the self in relationship to God and the world (of many cultures, wisdom traditions, disciplines, communities, etc.). Learning is not fully realized until it is articulated. Theological pedagogy will promote such articulation in ways that enhance experiential and dialogical learning.

Spirit-ed theological education does not just accept pedagogical connectivism and constructionism because they are popular or effective in a networked world. The dialogical principle of the Pentecost outpouring of the divine breath upon all two thousand years ago instead provides an explicitly theological rationale for consideration and implementation of such pedagogical approaches. If in former ages and eras seminary education prized withdrawal from society for the purposes of ecclesial and ministerial formation, our present interconnected era of online students already socially embedded in multiple time zones and missionally engaged in various ecclesial-cultural contexts invites retrieval of the early church's Pentecost experience that amplifies rather than silences the many voices coming from and going to the ends of the earth. As important, the *basileia* heralded by the Spirit norms our constructivism ethically so that the barriers keeping Jews and gentiles from appreciating each other's gifts can be surmounted and so that all can benefit from the fruits of the Spirit borne through those who come from many nations, cultures, and traditions.

Experiences of the Spirit: Inclusive and Embodied Learning

Whereas the preceding section focused on retrieving (from chap. 6 above) the dialogical aspect of theological education's transformational teleology, in the rest of this chapter I explore the pedagogical dimensions that undergird the devotional formation of persons-in-ecumenical-ecclesial-community. Here I examine the embodied and affective practices that drive theological pedagogy, and in the next section I consider the ensuing and correlated missional practices. My first question is how an embodied and affective education can be pedagogically facilitated.

One of the more comprehensive models addressing this cluster of questions in contemporary educational theory is intersectional pedagogy.[8] Intersectionality names the multiplicity internal to personal identities, focusing in particular on the nexus where race, gender, sexuality, class, and disability/ability meet. If Western culture has long presumed as normative the white, heterosexual, middle-class, nondisabled male, then intersectionality theory clarifies that, for instance, a lower-class, impoverished, and differently abled lesbian person of color deviates from the norm across all five registers and therefore suffers fivefold from sociocultural stigmatization and experiential exclusion. Now I understand that in at least one of these categorical dimensions—that concerning sexuality—there is no theological consensus regarding questions of identity since some people resist the idea that predispositions toward same-sex attractions are genetically prefigured. Regardless of those debates, there is no denying that non-heterosexual persons are often marginalized and victimized and that many, including and especially within the church, internalize wider (ecclesially supported) norms to the point of developing self-imprecated and oppressed identities, and it is this that ought to provide common cause for theological education, at least in the area of pastoral care and missional praxis.

Moreover, I understand that this discussion does not presume any type of reverse discrimination to suppress or exclude white, heterosexual, middle-class, and able-bodied males. Because theological education is supposed to be redemptive for all, especially for those historically underrepresented in this arena, there have to be pedagogical means for all learners to be intersectionally empowered in relational community.[9] What are the implications of such an intersectional pedagogy?

Feminist epistemologies and related pedagogies (note the deliberate plural here) have been particularly influential in identifying how the androcentricity dominant in some segments of the Western academy manifests the disembodied cognitivism that privileges theory over practice and that foregrounds the talking head at the expense of the whole person's experience. Observe how feminist epistemology invites a more embodied, relational, and participatory approach to learning.[10] What David Kelsey called the "Berlin" model, which prizes intellectual abstraction, is still considered by many the *modus operandi* of the Western university. But feminist theorizing roots speculative thought in embodied and affective experience. Similarly, individual achievements are still often prized above all others in academia. But feminist approaches foster collective and collaborative endeavors. In the same way, the modernist paradigm relies upon and even calcifies in some contexts the subject-object distinction. But feminist sensibilities note the interrelationality of subject and object, not only epistemologically but also ontologically, so that learners obtain their educational objectives both by adopting a detached posture (useful in some, if not many, contexts) and by personally engaging with, participating in, and even experiencing what they are studying. This is not to deny that academic feminism has also emerged out of the Enlightenment resistance against premodern hierarchicalism and authoritarianism, but it is to say that modernity's marginalizing of the body has been named and found wanting. In short, feminist pedagogical sensibilities and practices motivate the kind of experiential learning consistent with the main frames of the connected and constructivist educational environment coming into prominence in the present era.

Disability epistemologies and pedagogies have similar emphases, but I wish to tease out additional nuances. Of course, there are many types of impairments, and any single category includes a whole spectrum of experiences that caution against those with temporally able bodies drawing conclusions only from their own experiences. Persons with visual, audial, intellectual, or developmental impairments, as examples, will need pedagogical environments that embrace the ways they learn, since their learning might not involve the seeing, hearing, and discursive processing prevalent in mainstream classrooms. The point is that people across the spectrum of disabilities/abilities will learn differently than others, and that educational theory needs to be attentive to what some are calling a multisensorial pedagogy.[11] Here abstract cognitivism gives way to multisensory approaches that activate learning through seeing, touching, smelling, feeling, and doing, each considered relevant to the curricular content, the intended learning outcomes, and learners' capacities. In some respects, this is parallel to if not also an extension of the multiple intelligences pedagogy that highlights learner predispositions in one or more dimensions of thinking, whether spatial, kinesthetic, musical, interpersonal, linguistic, mathematical, etc.[12] Disability perspectives help us to realize that thinking is directly correlated with experiential and sensorial capacities and that this modulates across the disability/ability continuum. Ideally, disability ought to be treated as an aspect of diversity—and some theological educators are moving in this direction so as not to single out disability—but we are not quite there yet, so I did not want to overlook these points.[13] Yet my own approach remains thoroughly theological, based on observations in chapter 6 about the Spirit's audial, visual, and kinesthetic manifestation at Pentecost, a manifestation that we understand as conducive to developing a Spirit-ed theological pedagogy that engages, rather than ignores, the gamut of human (disability/ability) experience. The Spirit's redemption of embodiment applies to all persons, including those with all sorts of impairments, no matter how severe or profound.[14]

Our Pentecost pedagogy thus emphasizes both that the Spirit is poured out upon all flesh and that the Spirit gives gifts (1 Cor. 12:4–11) to each member of the body of Christ and the people of God, assuredly more so to those members deemed less honorable or worthy of being a conduit for those gifts (12:12–24). Incarnational and pentecostal teaching and learning hence democratize the classroom: the weakest links, so to speak, are just as important, if not more so, to the learning conversation as those perceived as having natural charisms, status, or worldly wisdom. (That was certainly how Saint Paul framed the dispensing of the spiritual gifts to the ecclesial body concerned with other, more conventional assessments of capacities; compare 1 Cor. 12 with 1:17–2:16).[15] A renewed theological education comes about by the divine wind, and such blowings are not ethereally spiritual but palpably tangible, through the bodies of diversely able and capable learners, revitalizing, reanimating, and restoring their voices, narratives, and witnesses so that the learning community is mutually edified.[16]

It nevertheless needs to be repeated that our prioritizing here of disability/ability experience and perspective is not another capitulation to contemporary political correctness regarding mainstreaming the voices of those long marginalized (whether by patriarchy or, in this case, by ableist cultures). Instead, again, our commitments remain theological and pneumatological, together. The Spirit gives many gifts to the various members of the one body of Christ, distributed as the divine breath wills to each one, no matter how socially acceptable or not, so that each can contribute to the faith, hope, and love of the whole in anticipation of the eschatological maturation of the people of God (see 1 Cor. 13:10–12). The eschatological goal thereby resounds through the many enfleshed tongues, gifts, and actions of the members of the Christic body. If civil and political society has led the way in being more inclusive of people with disabilities, the church ought to be repentant and then motivated to enact more than abstract policies. Hence, theological education ought to nurture welcoming spaces that enact social practices, communal relationships, and mutual belonging, which together combine to overcome the chasm between "us" (temporarily able-bodied people) and "them" (those with impairments).[17]

Diverse Communities of the Spirit: Justice Seeking and Performative Learning

If my proposed dialogical pedagogy is more discursively oriented, my proposed embodied approach to teaching and learning is more practically engaged. This opens up a deeper discussion of the performative dimension of our pedagogical vision, one that emphasizes that learning accrues not just through cogitation but also through practice. To be clear, the dialogical as pedagogical is not merely theoretical but a practically performed activity that involves ministerial and missional conversation partners. My focus will therefore be on practices of engagement that go beyond intellectual comprehension to experiential interaction.[18]

Here, I pick up an essential thread from the preceding discussion of feminist and disability contributions to pedagogy, the thread that addresses the patriarchal and ableist norms that marginalize and oppress nonconformists. Part of the point about feminist and disability approaches is not just to understand how sociocultural norms privilege certain bodies, experiences, and perspectives, but to work toward a more inclusive and just sociocultural order in these regards. Feminist pedagogical practices empower men and women to value and encourage the latter to live fully into their divinely authorized vocation; similarly, disability perspectives empower both temporally able-bodied and impaired persons to embrace the latter's flourishing in their divinely charted vocations. There is hence a fine line between teaching and scholarship, on the one hand, and advocacy and activism, on the other.[19] But theological commitments extend beyond abstract understandings to generate responsible, informed, and critical thinking wedded to participatory actions that are directed toward creating more inclusive, welcoming, and equitable communities and to heralding a more just society.[20]

What then are the kinds of practices that support crossover between teaching-learning-scholarship as traditionally conceived and activism involving community engagement and social transformation? A Spirit-ed pedagogical model, I suggest, is a holistic one that cuts across intellectual, spiritual, ecclesial, and missional practices. These are distinct, in some respects disparate, but in the task of theological education they are intertwined. Intellectual practices as historically understood surely include research, reading, and writing, etc., but if these are interconnected with our practices of scriptural meditation, prayer, devotional contemplation, and Christian witness, then we can develop the capacity to author public advocacy and opinion essays and policy proposals based on research and data (rather than be only ideologically driven) and also reflect these spiritual commitments.[21] The transformation of hearts goes hand in hand with the conversion of minds.

Similarly, the practices of congregating, Eucharist/sharing meals, and corporate worship on the one side and of service (to others), hospitality, evangelism, and reconciliation (with strangers) on the other side provide ecclesial and missional grounding for our lives as a whole and for our spiritual and intellectual sojourns more particularly.[22] More detailed consideration of such practices can certainly be invited into some courses and programs of theological study, but we would do well to seek occasions across the theological curriculum to interrogate practices while at the same time bringing them to bear on theoretical constructs. Theological education as a whole ought to bridge the classical divide between theory and practice so that the former can critically strengthen the latter while the latter (practices) can provide real-life experiences to fuel the former (intellectual theorization). This connects academic theory with faithful discipleship (Christian life and witness) and provides critical per-spective for a mutual conversation between the academy and the church.

Remember, however, that the goal is not just pedagogy for its own sake, nor practices for practices' sake. Rather, theological education as a whole, and its pedagogical apparatus more specif-ically, ought to serve the church's missional task of preparing for the coming divine rule and reign. This means that pedagogical practices ought to foster both the yearning for and the heralding of the form of the *basileia tou theou* manifest particularly in the life and teachings of Jesus of Nazareth, and as glimpsed within his earliest followers. Yet, the *that* of the apostolic witness is not only repeatable rather simplistically in our contexts in *this* world; instead, we must translate the apostolic message in ever-new sociohistorical spaces and times so that our performance of the gospel will be relevant and appropriate to its new contexts. The *how* of such translation and the shape of such performative practice lie necessarily at the center of the theological education enterprise. And since theological learners today, those enrolled in online courses and programs and in general, are more socially engaged than ever before, it should not be too difficult for teach-ers/instructors—colearners in a connectivist and constructivist world—to work pedagogically with students to create opportu-nities that contextually link and appropriately relate curricular content with concrete action to shape the world.

Although contemporary philosophy of education has for some time been repairing the breach between theory and prac-tice opened up especially by the Enlightenment, the goal of this discussion is again to suggest that these insights have apostolic resonance (if not grounding). Of course, the apostolic authors were not pedagogues in the late modern sense, but their incarna-tional and pentecostal paradigm is firmly rooted in the Hebraic epistemology of embodied practice. Saint Luke thus narrates the early Christian story, attempting to provide historical perspec-tive and description but all the while communicating theological (and pneumatological) convictions and, most importantly, nurturing a missiological imagination.[23] He (and the other writers of the Christian testament) did not see Christian teaching and practice in binary terms. We know the truth in part because we act truth out, and this insight is pedagogically sound not only because contemporary educational theory tells us so.

In this chapter I have looked at the *how* of theological education: its pedagogical dimension. My emphasis has been on a dialogical, embodied, inclusive, and performative pedagogy amid a networked field. Such teaching and learning are less a science than an art. I am talking not about the five steps that produce certain results but about a range of teaching-learning practices that habituates our character for living out a faithful witness in a dynamic and complex world. We are thus praying for the wisdom of the Spirit that leads to truth in a way that prompts perceptive responses to the interrelationality of our lives amid a shifting flux.[24] The cultivation of such a theologically informed and spiritually grounded approach nurtures the sapiential and practical know-how that enables ongoing discrimination and judgment amid life's unpredictable twists and turns.[25] A Spirit-ed theological education is thus less about certifying content experts (after all, knowledge becomes dated so quickly in the information age) than about creating lifelong learners who grow in adaptive knowledge and ongoing dialogical, inclusive, and performative conversation.

Theological Scholarship

Renewing the Mind through the Spirit

Our movement in this book has been from the heart (the *who*), through the hands (the *why*), and now to the putative "head" of theological education, the intellectual aspects of *how* theological education achieves its tasks. More specifically, we are looking at the ways that theological education shapes the church for missional participation in a networked world. In this final part, focused on the intellectual work considered to be at the center of theological education, we have once again divided our discussion into a triadic frame: beginning with the curriculum, shifting to the pedagogy, and turning finally to the scholarly enterprise. Our argument throughout is that the life of the mind in theological education is not separate from but intimately interwoven with life in the Spirit.

In this final chapter I suggest that we think of scholarship less as a noun and more as a verb. If our teaching seeks to invite learners into a lifetime of theological inquiry, our scholarship invites a wider set of publics—for every person is potentially a reader of our books or blogs or other intellectual productions—into moments of theological reflection and reconsideration. The work of research and scholarly production emerges best out of a dynamically enabled participation in the movements of the divine breath, thereby orienting thoughtful reflexivity engaging the academy, the church, and the world, sometimes separately but also together in differentiated ways. How do we allow our ecclesial and missional experiences to raise research questions and prompt scholarly inquiry? How do we bring theoretical tools to bear on our ecclesial and missional efforts? How is theological scholarship triadically constituted at the nexus where academic, ecclesial, and missional sites converge?

The following pages conclude this book by exploring the scholarship of a theological faculty and its role for Spirit-ed theological education. In some respects, this is ground zero of theological education, and from this vantage point we can see how our scholarship affects our teaching and learning, and beyond that how it influences the church and its missional activity. We should imagine the scholarly endeavor as having ripple effects back out to where we connect with students in classrooms, with members of the body of Christ in churches, and with fellow human creatures in a world sustained by the divine breath.

Research amid the Academy: Eschatological Transdisciplinarity

The Enlightenment ideal was research and scholarship for its own sake, to advance knowledge not beholden to external interests that could compromise the course of inquiry with political, economic, or private motivation. In theory, such a framing of scholarly research with critical distance between the investigator and the subject studied was needed to ensure academic integrity. Further, the researcher was committed to determining the truth of the matter under inquiry, even if the results were neither fashionable nor particularly welcomed. Last but not least, there is the sense that the discipline of scholarship was itself a virtue, and that the scholar would also be recognized as having an honorable character. In short, there are various aspects of this ideal of the modern researcher and scholar—dispassionate in personality, methodical in practice, and virtuous in his or her way of life—that we ought not to dismiss in our networked era. Yet the present situation challenges this ideal not only because of its economic unsustainability but also because it sees the autonomous individual as an abstraction from our interrelatedness (with colleagues, students and fellow learners, and others in our various communities of inquiry).

I suggest instead a Spirit-ed approach to scholarship that includes theological warrants undergirding the quest for truth, such as the pneumatological engine driving that quest (e.g., the inspiration of the Spirit of truth), and a theological vision for the life of the mind, such as a pneumatological theology of wisdom framing the intellectual life (e.g., the disposition of the Spirit of wisdom). But I also suggest nesting such scholarship communally in ever-wider circles of embeddedness, starting with the faculty and expanding in whatever order makes sense to the respective guilds, churches, and wider publics.

Now perhaps you can see how the twenty-first-century networked world both extends the research trajectory in many directions at once and also complicates its evaluation. This mirrors the growing normativity of interdisciplinarity in scholarly research and the diminishing chasm between facts and values that is characteristic of what some term postmodern scholarship. I noted at the end of chapter 7 that the theological curriculum is increasingly interdisciplinary, or at least ought to be, to take up the questions of our time more adequately. Similarly, if two generations ago doctoral research was characterized first and foremost by drilling deep in a narrow area, today such projects are widening. What are becoming much more prevalent are research projects that cross disciplinary boundaries, that forge new pathways of inquiry on disciplinary margins or tangents, that bring perspectives from one field or domain of inquiry to bear on another, and that deploy theoretical and analytical tools from one arena to engage with realities and questions in another. The hermeneutical character of all inquiry means that research proceeds less in a straight line than from sphere to sphere or from dot to dot, each location adding new insights into the mix, reconfiguring prior (perhaps settled) conclusions, and prompting fresh reconsiderations. Put differently, since every topic can be pursued from a fresh angle, adoption of new disciplinary tools and perspectives is now one of the primary ways that knowledge is pushed forward.

All of this is not only consonant with our Spirit-ed hermeneutical and methodological stance but can perhaps cautiously be said to be contemporary expressions of the Spirit's ongoing work. I would simply invite theological educators to conscientiously discern the work of the Spirit and ask how we can more intentionally participate in that activity. The Pentecost narrative that frames the educational paradigm in this book insists on nothing less than an ongoing and ever-expanding dialogue crossing every preconceived or conventional boundary, not the least of which are the disciplinary silos that have long divided the modern research academy. The renewal of theological scholarship brought about by the Spirit involves what will be a radical mutuality: theological disciplines reaching out to and receiving the gifts (and tongues) of other scholarly disciplines and then also contributing theological questions and perspectives in the languages (and tongues) of these others. The unity of knowledge, for us a theologically/pneumatologically grounded conviction, invites—even demands—such a dynamic and dialogical stance committed to inquiry for the long haul.[1] All considerations are provisional and fallible, not necessarily in the sense that they can somehow be overturned outright and dismissed in toto, but in the sense that they can be elaborated upon, revised, or deepened in light of new perspectives. This is how the Spirit's many tongues declare the glory of God over time in theological scholarship.

What of the teleological and especially axiological dimension of scholarship that complicates this discussion? The modern ideal was that the so-called *facts* needed to speak for themselves, unvarnished by our preferred evaluations; early modern naturalistic commitments urged that nature's objective realities and truth ought to be distinguished from humanity's subjective feelings and biases. Our late modern context, however, has shown that there is no human knowledge of the reality or truth in itself without our involvement, and that all facts are value-laden, or at least engaged from our situatedness or perspective.[2] At least for those committed to Christian discipleship, this opens up to missional witness. And the Christian scholar, in this instance, is also in some respects a preacher, proclaiming the good news (*kērygma*) of the coming reign of God.[3] Such scholarship is meant not just to inform but also to persuade, to inspire, and even to impel. At the least, such scholarly productivity is designed to herald the coming *basileia tou theou* while being both conscious of and conscientious about its Christian credentials and respectful of those who have others. Hence, such scholarship is not neutral in its commitments or its agenda but engages the public square and its pluralism according to what has been revealed about the coming *basileia* in the life and teachings of Jesus and his followers.

It is in these senses that I am suggesting how theological scholarship is mutually eschatological and transdisciplinary. The life of the mind participates in and is invigorated by the Spirit of Pentecost, which makes present the message of Jesus in a multiplicity of languages and discourses. The intellectual life is most robust, we believe, when it is pneumatically animated. This is not to say that theological scholarship has to be filled with ecclesial jargon. It is to say that the Spirit-filled scholarly endeavor will be empowered to bear witness to the God of Jesus Christ, but in and through the particularity of the languages customary in the various contexts within which such scholarship unfolds. There may be more mainstream academic projects centered in established disciplinary spheres, more exploratory inquiry on the disciplinary margins, or more inter- and transdisciplinary engagements, and each will retain the specificity of its discursive tradition, albeit pushing the discussion forward in following (from the Christian perspective) the Spirit's leading into all truth. Each generation expands the discussion further in this or that direction, and the next generation picks up the baton, having also received the promise of the same Spirit (Acts 2:39). The eschatological character of such inquiry means that the final word is always coming, which prompts wonder, piques curiosity, and sustains research—and so supplies exactly what funds theological scholarship.

Scholarship by and for the Church: Ecumenical Ecclesiality

Let me put some major caveats on the table at the onset of this discussion about scholarship by and for the church. First, although theological educators will generally understand themselves as members of the body of Christ (with the exception of the very small number of theologians who have the scholarly and academic expertise but not faith commitments), many have honed their scholarly gifts for engaging academia and devoted their life's work in that direction rather than toward writing for the church. Not that *all* theological educators need to write for the church—although if no or very few members of a theological faculty did, we would wonder about how ecclesially connected that group of scholars is and whether they are effective in educating learners, the vast majority of whom will not be professional theologians. Any theological faculty should have some members both able and willing to engage the church in their scholarship, and the system of theological education ought to encourage and reward such efforts.

Further, then, if we allowed any number of our colleagues to write only academically (the above point), might we agree that another set, those more professionally rather than academically engaged, would wish to write mostly for the church? This may in fact be the practical outcome of having PhD and professional doctoral tracks in any theological faculty: that we'll have the "scholars" gathered in the former, producing for fellow academics, and the "practitioners" leading the latter, writing ecclesially. Our Spirit-ed theological paradigm, however, intends to recognize the integrity and interdependence of both domains: there are legitimate places for scholarly inquiry and ecclesial engagement, but the latter ought to be informed by research and scholarship even as the former ought to be cognizant of broader implications. Going forward, then, there should be less and less bifurcation between the two and more and more valuation of their interrelatedness, even if individual faculty members may tend in their ongoing scholarship to address one of these spheres more than the other. A cohesive theological faculty will recognize the multiple gifts and accents and be able to honor such work in both their scholarly and ecclesial forms. Ideally, we would have practitioners that write with theoretical rigor who also have the ability to interrogate theoretical schemes from their practical positionality, as well as scholars who take the time to write in ways accessible to broader (nonacademic) audiences. This would both test the viability of theory in the real world and sharpen Christian praxis.

When we turn to address the character of scholarship for the church, we can also realize its heterogeneity. Beyond discovery of new knowledge (the traditional form of academic scholarship), there are integration with other areas, application to the real world, and the formation of other publics, in this case the church.[4] Theological educators can write in these latter forms for church leaders, for broader (mass) consumption, and for everything in between. These are blurred categories to begin with, as part 1 of this book sought to illuminate. But we can nevertheless use these as heuristic descriptions of audiences to tease out the nature of ecclesial scholarship.

What is entailed in writing for ecclesial leadership? It certainly means attention to the clergy, even hierarchically organized in episcopal traditions, although in our postdenominational world this may be a shrinking class or one that will continue to adapt in such radical ways as to provoke questions of continuity with past understandings. Rather than official leaders, we might wish to address those committed to the tasks of ecclesial witness, for instance, the Pauline delineation of apostolic, prophetic, evangelistic, pastoral, and teaching activities that "equip the saints for the work of ministry, for building up the body of Christ" (Eph. 4:11–12). If we consider this a nonexhaustive list, we can envision identifying new tasks at the vanguard of what the church is becoming—the formation of digital communities of faith and practice, for instance (see chap. 3 above)—and then write for those at the forefront of such efforts. Perhaps this might be a kind of *how-to* manual, but hopefully, the practicalities of such proposals will be undergirded by exacting research, critical scholarship, and robust theological reflection.

Similarly, writing for the so-called laity in the twenty-first century will be more challenging since they are a more expansive group than in the Christendom of the past, which clearly defined the distinctions between them and their clerical counterparts. If there are bi-vocational pastors that break the stereotypical role of clergy in our networked world, there are also laity who are ministerially and missionally engaged and who even consider this aspect of their lifework or work life to be of greater consequence than their so-called day job. Further, members of the body of Christ and of the fellowship of the Spirit in the present time are more educated than the traditional laity of generations past, and that greater education on a wider range of issues will invite if not require more effective translations of theological scholarship to sustain their engagement. We are not just talking about theological educators writing devotional tracts; instead, we are envisioning how theologians can bring their scholarly perspectives to the church in all its diversity in order to "equip the saints for the work of ministry, for building up the body of Christ," as Saint Paul put it. How can Christian scholarship help twenty-first-century believers navigating multiple borders, connections, and crisscrossings of a radically connected world make sense of their identity in Christ and live out their missional witness in the Spirit?

Such scholarship for the church will need to be deeply ecumenical, richly pentecostal, and radically evangelical. For while denominational labels will carry less and less weight going forward, the church needs to understand itself in its changing forms and contexts, and nothing less is required than Spirit-led retrieval (which is not equivalent to repetition without differences) from its wellsprings across Protestant, Catholic, and Orthodox traditions for missional purposes. Thus the radicality of the good news is its capacity to make a difference to today's networked humanity according to the shape of the coming divine rule heralded in Jesus's life and words. Theological educators are more needed than ever before to help the church and its leaders not only survive these challenges but flourish.

Many Tongues, Many Peers, and Many Referees: Witnessing in and with the World

In the end, then, theological educators are interested not just in theory for its own sake but also in teaching, learning, and producing scholarship that contributes to the church's mission in a networked world. And what is that mission again? It is participation in the message and work of Jesus, the one filled with the Spirit, to announce the coming divine rule in the present age. As missiologist and historian Andrew Walls puts it, "The pursuit of the scholarly life is a Christian vocation within God's mission to the world."[5] This missional horizon covers the church's interface with the world in its geographic expansiveness—to the ends of the earth, in Luke's words—and its multidimensionality: the interconnected social, cultural, religious, economic, political, and environmental spheres. If modern universities pursue the knowledges pertinent to and important for think tanks, research firms, development nongovernmental organizations, transnational organizations, and state and other information agencies,[6] institutions of theological education have both the opportunity and the challenge to contribute theologically relevant perspectives for the common planetary good.

It is unthinkable, of course, that any one faculty member can expertly address all the diverse arenas and their various constituencies with any depth and nuance. That is why theological faculties are put together, ideally, in ways that enable members to develop competencies in one or another direction while allowing colleagues to chart distinct areas of expertise and interest. Theological educators of the future will need to hone translation skills that bring theological themes and principles into other domains in relevant ways, not only to avoid the specter of trespassing on the scholarly territories guarded by other experts but also to avoid the embarrassment of pontificating on topics upon which they lack the necessary knowledge to expound.[7] Thus, theological scholarship for "the world" usually emerges over time: improvisationally nurtured by expanding life experiences in ever-wider circles of public engagement, theological educators grow in their capacity to produce scholarship that is both fluent and credible with "worldly" audiences.[8]

We are talking in some respects of what traditionally has been named the public intellectual. There are some models of theologians who have been public intellectuals. For some, Reinhold Niebuhr is the classic exemplar, for others Cornel West has set the recent standard, and for the rest of us there are other models. But theological scholarship for the world is an increasingly rare commodity, sidelined both by the marginalization of theological schools, departments, and faculties from the public square of universities and by the privatization of religion in late modern public life.[9] So, the trick is not just to attempt to be an evangelist outside of ecclesial domains (although in one sense, that is what scholarship for the world is about) but also to recognize that we as theological educators both should not pretend that we are other than theological in our heart of hearts and that at the end of the day we are witnessing to the impending divine reign. Yet, if theological education nevertheless ought to engage the public square (and this book is premised in part on this obligation), then theologians will also need to develop as public intellectuals, at least in being able to address public topics from theological perspectives. Indeed, might it even be possible that theologians can contribute to and further redefine the nature of public intellectualism currently being renegotiated?[10]

The traditional mode of scholarship that "counts" (for academic tenure and advancement) is academic books in university presses and articles in peer-reviewed journals. While nothing in this discussion presumes that these be discontinued, we ought to recognize two emerging trends: that peer review works differently in different domains, and that scholarship that counts ought not to be limited to these historic genres. We suggested earlier that scholarship produced for ecclesial audiences will not take the form of the scholarly monograph or the technical article. It takes just as much skill to write books and essays for the church in its diversity of forms, expressions, and manifestations. Similarly, writing for the public square requires and invites a diversified approach. Theological educators who engage these various audiences will need to tailor their contributions to find reception in the relevant venues. Few theologians will gain a second PhD to be able to write a monograph that can pass peer review in a book series in that other disciplinary environment. But more and more can and ought to bring theological perspectives to bear on matters of public concern, even as we as theologically oriented scholars ought to welcome the questions and input of those working in these other areas about our theological discourses. This is the dialogical mutuality at the heart of a renewed theological education in a networked world: theological scholarship witnesses to, and thus engages, the public square, even as the voices in the public domain in some sense speak back to the theological guild, and through that to the church. The "witness" is thus reciprocal.

How does this actually work? It works through the many forms of scholarship that reach out from the theological academy into the world, and that are in fact open and accessible to the breadth of audiences that theological scholars might wish to address or hope to persuade. I do not mean to suggest that blogging or other expressions of digital scholarship seeking to engage broader publics should displace the scholarly article.[11] But I do mean to argue that digital scholarship ought not to be dismissed as a valuable part of the larger package that emerges over the course of a theological educator's scholarly journey, especially if such exercises can be shown to be a consistent extension of one's scholarly work that also fulfills institutional vision and mission objectives. Put otherwise, the theological academy ought to recognize that its members will speak in many tongues and that their scholarship will appear in many genres.

Patterns are important here: the "peers" that review and referee one's blog, opinion articles, policy proposals, or other so-called popular writings are of course not academic peers. Again, it is not that the latter are unimportant—and there is much to be said in ongoing defense of the double-blind review processes operative in the theological academy—but we ought to consider how peer review operates differently in different communities and recognize that manifold review processes are at work in the real (networked) world in our own assessments and evaluation of our peers as producers of scholarship. The church will review the value of our contributions variously, and this will lead to further invitations to speak or write over time . . . or not. Similarly, theological materials that engage the wider public square will be evaluated in these domains by those having interest and greater (or lesser) degrees of relevant expertise. Assuming that these works are accessible to their intended audiences—a point often overlooked but increasingly highlighted by calls for open-source and open-access publication even within academia[12]—ecclesial and public engagement and response will provide in themselves a kind of check and balance, feedback loop, albeit relevant to different "communities of accountability in and beyond the academy."[13] Hence it is not that there is no peer review in place for such publications, but that it operates a bit differently than the formalized academic referee process. The analogy in the latter arena is the capacity to count citations given developing technologies; similar criteria can be workable in ecclesial and public domains, albeit correlated not just with actual "hits" or "visits" (e.g., to any website) but to the arc of reception that can be demonstrated about how one's theological scholarship is both being translated into other media and received by these various constituencies. Demonstration that one continues to be invited to engage in the public sphere can give a tenure and promotion committee added evidence (still in need of critical evaluation, of course) of effective scholarship in and for a networked world.

What we are calling for is an opening up of evaluative schemes for promotion and tenure in a more pluralistic direction. Such pluralism can be operative at different levels and in different contexts. In any one faculty, some members might demonstrate their excellence by one set of metrics and others might demonstrate excellence by other nonmutually exclusive sets. Different institutions might value and deploy multiple assessments in different ways. Theological educators are already operating according to manifold criteria, including those set in their guilds and those set by their ecclesial communities, and even these two sets are not mutually exclusive. The call here is simply to recognize that different, indeed many fragmented and overlapping, publics are already engaged with theological thinking and that our scholarship, vocationally developed in these various directions, also ought to be variously assessed.

It is in this context that we can say something else about academic freedom. Such freedom of speech and inquiry is fundamentally contextual, enabled and constrained by the development of discursive traditions, ecclesial commitments, historical circumstances, cosmo-political situatedness, and rhetorical and communicative intentions. Ultimately, our freedoms are sustained by the divine breath and lured by the discernible form of the coming *basileia tou theou* so that on some occasions we will need to speak truth to (academic, ecclesial, or worldly) power and may suffer reactionary consequences, while on other occasions we comfort, encourage, and instill possibilities in the face of despair. We are free to follow the blowings of the divine wind, and what to produce and how to present it are to be discerned at each juncture in considering the power of the Spirit vis-à-vis the powers that be.

In the end, we arrive in some ways back at the beginning: affirming that theological scholarship, an expression of the intellectual life, is also intrinsic to life in the Spirit, and that such a Spirit-led endeavor engages the scholarly academy and the church and its witness to the world about the coming divine rule. Theology itself, rather than being one, is many, at least manifest in and through the many tongues of the Spirit, and hence edifies the many forms and expressions of the church in the many contexts in which she bears witness. Institutions of theological education seeking to thrive in today's flat world ought not to neglect the potential of being reinvigorated by specifically theological resources. This book has suggested one such theological horizon—that informed by the Pentecost narrative of the Spirit's outpouring upon all flesh.

For Further Thought

Those interested in pursuing further the ideas presented in this book are invited to consult the reference works in the endnotes. I also highly recommend the other eleven books in this Theological Education between the Times series that this book is a part of, a good number of which have also been referred to in the endnotes.

Notes

Preface

1. In this book I capitalize "Pentecost" when referring to the Lukan Day of Pentecost and "Pentecostal" when referring to proper names of churches or to the modern movement going by that name, but I do not capitalize the adjective "pentecostal."

Introduction

1. Thomas L. Friedman, *The World Is Flat: A Brief History of the Twenty-First Century*, 3rd ed. (New York: Farrar, Straus & Giroux, 2007).

2. Manuel Castells, *The Information Age: Economy, Society, and Culture*, 3 vols. (Oxford: Blackwell, 1996–1998).

3. Yochai Benkler, *The Wealth of Networks: How Social Production Transforms Markets and Freedom* (New Haven: Yale University Press, 2006).

4. E.g., Henry C. Lucas Jr., *Technology and the Disruption of Higher Education* (Singapore: World Scientific, 2016), and Toru Iiyoshi and M. S. Vijay Kumar, eds., *Opening Up Education: The Collective Advancement of Education through Open Technology, Open Content, and Open Knowledge* (Cambridge, MA: MIT Press, 2010).

5. E.g., Edward Farley, *The Fragility of Knowledge: Theological Education in the Church and the University* (Philadelphia: Fortress, 1988); David H. Kelsey, *To Understand God Truly: What's Theological about a Theological School* (Louisville: Westminster John Knox, 1992).

6. This formulation is indebted to Swiss pedagogue Johann Pestalozzi (1746–1827). See Arthur Brühlmeier, *Head, Heart, and Hand: Education in*

the Spirit of Pestalozzi (Cambridge: Sophia, 2010); Perry Shaw, *Transforming Theological Education: A Practical Handbook for Integrative Learning* (Carlisle, UK: Langham Global Library, 2014), 31–33.

7. See L. Gregory Jones, "Beliefs, Desires, Practices, and the Ends of Theological Education," in *Practicing Theology: Beliefs and Practices in Christian Life*, ed. Miroslav Volf and Dorothy C. Bass (Grand Rapids: Eerdmans, 2002), 185–205, and Matthias Wenk, "Do We Need a Distinctive European Pentecostal/Charismatic Approach to Theological Education?," *Journal of the European Pentecostal Theological Association* 23 (2003): 58–71.

Chapter 1

1. I am grateful to Chris Meinzer at ATS for much of the data in this section. D. E. "Gene" Mills Jr., at the Dixon Pentecostal Research Center, which is affiliated with the Pentecostal Theological Seminary of the Church of God, Cleveland, Tennessee, helped with some of the statistics for pentecostal churches and denominations.

2. One caution is essential at this moment: my use of "evangelical" is not meant as oppositional to "mainline Protestant"; as shall be clear in the rest of this chapter, the latter is not homogeneous and includes various evangelical thrusts and expressions, even as the former can be understood as a form of Christian life rather than as encrusted in institutionalized structures. Surely there are organized evangelical churches that exist also as denominational bureaucracies.

3. John H. Leith, *Crisis in the Church: The Plight of Theological Education* (Louisville: Westminster John Knox, 1997); Maria Erling, "Futures for Mainline Protestant Institutions," in *The Future of Mainline Protestantism in America*, ed. James Hudnut-Beumler and Mark Silk (New York: Columbia University Press, 2018), 97–100.

4. The numbers in this paragraph derive from the Pew Research Center's "America's Changing Religious Landscape," May 12, 2015, http://www.pew forum.org/2015/05/12/americas-changing-religious-landscape/. Hereafter, page references from this work will be given in parentheses in the text by the word "Pew," followed by the page number.

5. I have extrapolated these numbers from the data given to me by Meinzer and Mills (see n. 1) and then connected them with those of denominational and other sources easily available on the Internet.

6. Although above I did not comment on the Southern Baptist Convention (SBC), since it represents a distinct kind of evangelicalism that deserves

separate treatment, this group that features a dozen or so theological seminaries is experiencing decline in ways that mirror wider trends among evangelical and pentecostal churches that have their origins in the early twentieth century; see, e.g., Travis Loller, "Southern Baptists See 12th Year of Declining Membership," *Religion News Service*, May 24, 2019, https://re ligionnews.com/2019/05/24/southern-baptists-see-12th-year-of-declining -membership/. Thanks to Ted Smith for this source.

7. Ted Smith's book in this series expertly situates this so-called narrative of decline in broader historical and cultural context in order for us to appreciate the constructive possibilities yet latent in the present horizon.

8. E.g., Candy Gunther Brown, "Conclusion," in *The Future of Evangelicalism in America*, ed. Candy Gunther Brown and Mark Silk (New York: Columbia University Press, 2016), 203–23.

9. After I settled on the title for this section, I noticed that James Hudnut-Beumler, in "Conclusion: The Quakerization of Mainline Protestantism," in Hudnut-Beumler and Silk, *The Future of Mainline Protestantism in America*, 190–93, uses "evangelicalization" to speak about trends in mainline Protestantism. My usage is being applied to theological education apart from but not unrelated to his observations.

10. See https://www.nae.net/.

11. David Bebbington, "Evangelicalism in Modern Britain and America: A Comparison," in *Amazing Grace: Evangelicalism in Australia, Britain, Canada, and the United States*, ed. George A. Rawlyk and Mark A. Noll (Grand Rapids: Baker Books, 1993), 185.

12. See https://www.ats.edu/member-schools for these categorizations.

13. See also Mark Young's book in this series, which provides another perspective on evangelical theological education.

14. Mark Labberton, *Still Evangelical? Insiders Consider Political, Social, and Theological Meaning* (Downers Grove, IL: IVP, 2018).

15. Derek Penwell, *The Mainliner's Survival Guide to the Post-Denominational World* (St. Louis: Chalice, 2014).

16. Brown, "Conclusion," 205–7.

17. Eddie Gibbs and Ian Coffey, *Church Next: Quantum Changes in Christian Ministry* (Leicester, UK: Inter-Varsity, 2000), chaps. 3–4.

18. Brad Christerson and Richard Flory, *The Rise of Network Christianity: How Independent Leaders Are Changing the Religious Landscape* (Oxford: Oxford University Press, 2017).

19. Vincent W. Lloyd, *In Defense of Charisma* (New York: Columbia University Press, 2018).

20. Andy Lord, *Network Church: A Pentecostal Ecclesiology Shaped by Mission* (Leiden: Brill, 2012).

21. See Mark A. Noll and James Turner, *The Future of Christian Learning: An Evangelical and Catholic Dialogue*, ed. Thomas Albert Howard (Grand Rapids: Brazos, 2008).

22. Amos Yong and Vinson Synan, eds., *Global Renewal Christianity: Spirit-Empowered Movements Past, Present, and Future*, 4 vols. (Lake Mary, FL: Charisma, 2016–2017).

23. Also Veli-Matti Kärkkäinen, *Toward a Pneumatological Theology: Pentecostal and Ecumenical Perspectives on Ecclesiology, Soteriology, and Theology of Mission*, ed. Amos Yong (Lanham, MD: University Press of America, 2002), chap. 8.

24. See Amos Yong, *Renewing Christian Theology: Systematics for a Global Christianity*, images and commentary by Jonathan A. Anderson (Waco, TX: Baylor University Press, 2014), chap. 7.

25. Letty M. Russell, "Ecumenical Theological Education and God's Pentecostal Gift," *Ministerial Formation* 87 (1999): 14–23.

Chapter 2

1. What I attempt in this chapter is also considered, but from a very different angle, in Maria Liu Wong's book in this series.

2. Pew Research Center, "America's Changing Religious Landscape," May 12, 2015, 52, http://www.pewforum.org/2015/05/12/americas-changing-re ligious-landscape/. Hereafter, page references from this work will be given in parentheses in the text by the word "Pew," followed by the page number.

3. Roberto Chao Romero, *Brown Church: Five Centuries of Latina/o Social Justice, Theology, and Identity* (Downers Grove, IL: IVP Academic, 2020).

4. E.g., Estrelda Y. Alexander and Amos Yong, eds., *Afro-Pentecostalism: Black Pentecostal and Charismatic Christianity in History and Culture*, Religion, Race, and Ethnicity Series (New York: New York University Press, 2011).

5. See also Keri Day's book in this series. Day focuses on theological education in the black church tradition in general and in the Afro-pentecostal churches more particularly.

6. See David D. Daniels, "African Immigrant Churches in the United States and the Study of Black Church History," in *African Immigrant Religions in America*, ed. Jacob K. Olupona and Regina Gemignani (New York: New York University Press, 2007), 47–60; cf. Afe Adogame, *The African Christian*

Diaspora: New Currents and Emerging Trends in World Christianity (London: Bloomsbury, 2013).

7. I am grateful to Rev. Andrews Donkor, Regional Head (Apostle) of the Church of Pentecost in Los Angeles, for the current figures.

8. See Allison Norton, "Migrant-Shaped Urban Mission: The Missionary Nature and Initiatives of the Church of Pentecost, USA," in *Working Papers of the American Society of Missiology*, vol. 2, *Third Wave Mission/Migration*, ed. Robert A. Danielson and William L. Selvidge (Wilmore, KY: First Fruits, 2016), 72.

9. I am grateful for this information about the church, obtained through Nimi Wariboko, a prolific social ethicist and holder of the Walter Muelder Chair in Social Ethics at Boston University's School of Theology, who has also served as RCCG missionary and pastor, and currently is chair of the board of trustees for the Redeemed Christian Bible College and Seminary.

10. Darrin J. Rodgers, "Assemblies of God 2014 Statistics Released, Reveals Ethnic Transformation," Flower Pentecostal Heritage Center, June 18, 2015, https://ifphc.wordpress.com/2015/06/18/assemblies-of-god-2014 -statistics-released-reveals-ethnic-transformation/.

11. Elizabeth Conde-Frazier's book in this series unpacks the diversity of Latino/a communities vis-à-vis theological education; see also Conde-Frazier, *Hispanic Bible Institutes: A Community of Theological Construction* (Scranton, PA: University of Scranton Press, 2004).

12. The Asociación para la Educación Teológica Hispana accredits certificates, and perhaps in part for this reason does not send as many students on to graduate programs, even if ATS schools have worked out an agreement to accept such certificate students as having the educational equivalent of the bachelor's degree.

13. Rudy Estrada, "Renewing Theological Education: Developing Networks of Latino/a Ethnocultural Inclusion," *PentecoStudies: An Interdisciplinary Journal for Research on the Pentecostal & Charismatic Movements* 17, no. 2 (2018): 134–57.

14. See also Arlene M. Sánchez Walsh, *Latino Pentecostal Identity: Evangelical Faith, Self, and Society* (New York: Columbia University Press, 2003), chap. 2.

15. Kenneth Davis and Edwin I. Hernandez, eds., *Reconstructing the Sacred Tower: Challenge and Promise of Latino/a Theological Education*, Hispanic Theological Initiative Series 3 (Scranton, PA: University of Scranton Press, 2003), chap. 3; Katarina Schuth, *Seminary Formation: Recent History, Current Circumstances, New Directions* (Collegeville, MN: Liturgical Press, 2016). See

also Hoffsman Ospino's book on theological education in the Roman Catholic world in this series.

16. E.g., Roberto Chao Romero, *The Chinese in Mexico, 1882–1940* (Tucson: University of Arizona Press, 2010).

17. See Chloe Sun's book on Logos Evangelical Seminary in this series.

18. Todd M. Johnson and Kenneth R. Ross, eds., *Atlas of Global Christianity, 1910–2010* (Edinburgh: Edinburgh University Press, 2009), 53.

19. Philip Jenkins, *The Next Christendom: The Coming of Global Christianity* (Oxford: Oxford University Press, 2002) and *The New Faces of Christianity: Believing the Bible in the Global South* (Oxford: Oxford University Press, 2006).

20. Yŏng-gi Hong, "Encounter with Modernity: The 'McDonaldization' and 'Charismatization' of Korean Mega-Churches," *International Review of Mission* 92, no. 365 (2003): 239–55; Henri Paul Pierre Gooren, "The Pentecostalization of Religion and Society in Latin America," *Exchange* 39, no. 4 (2010): 355–76; Moritz Fischer, "'The Spirit Helps Us in Our Weakness': Charismatization of Worldwide Christianity and the Quest for an Appropriate Pneumatology with Focus on the Evangelical Lutheran Church in Tanzania," *Journal of Pentecostal Theology* 20, no. 1 (2011): 95–121.

21. See Dietrich Werner et al., eds., *Handbook of Theological Education in World Christianity: Theological Perspectives, Ecumenical Trends, Regional Surveys* (Eugene, OR: Wipf & Stock, 2010).

22. The Global Directory of Theological Education Institutions enumerates over seven thousand such institutions, departments, and faculties around the world; see https://www.globethics.net/web/gtl/directory/search.

23. Samuel Escobar, *The New Global Mission: The Gospel from Everywhere to Everyone* (Downers Grove, IL: IVP Academic, 2003), and Allen Yeh, *Polycentric Missiology: 21st-Century Mission from Everyone to Everywhere* (Downers Grove, IL: IVP Academic, 2016).

24. See Paul Freston, "Reverse Mission: A Discourse in Search of Reality?," *PentecoStudies* 9, no. 2 (2010): 153–74.

25. See Amos Yong, *The Spirit Poured Out on All Flesh: Pentecostalism and the Possibility of Global Theology* (Grand Rapids: Baker Academic, 2005), chap. 5.

26. See Jerome Crowe, *From Jerusalem to Antioch: The Gospel across Cultures* (Collegeville, MN: Liturgical Press, 1997), chap. 13.

27. Paul Trebilco, *The Early Christians in Ephesus from Paul to Ignatius* (Grand Rapids: Eerdmans, 2007), chap. 6.

Chapter 3

1. See Michael Welker, *God the Spirit*, trans. John M. Hoffmeyer (Minneapolis: Fortress, 1994), chap. 5.

2. Stanley M. Burgess, *Christian Peoples of the Spirit: A Documentary History of Pentecostal Spirituality from the Early Church to the Present* (New York: New York University Press, 2011).

3. See David J. Courey, *What Has Wittenberg to Do with Azusa? Luther's Theology of the Cross and Pentecostal Triumphalism* (New York: T&T Clark, 2016), part 1.

4. E.g., Christian Smith with Patricia Snell, *Souls in Transition: The Religious and Spiritual Lives of Emerging Adults* (Oxford: Oxford University Press, 2009), 287–92.

5. Pew Research Center, "America's Changing Religious Landscape," May 12, 2015, 30, http://www.pewforum.org/2015/05/12/americas-changing-religious-landscape/.

6. See James Emery White, *The Rise of the Nones: Understanding and Reaching the Religiously Unaffiliated* (Grand Rapids: Baker Books, 2014), 27.

7. Pew Research Center, "America's Changing Religious Landscape," 43. What we see in the Southern Baptist Convention plays itself out across the North American denominational and ecclesial landscape; see Ryan P. Burge, "Only Half of Kids Raised Southern Baptist Stay Southern Baptist," *Christianity Today*, May 24, 2019, https://www.christianitytoday.com/news/2019/may/southern-baptist-sbc-decline-conversion-retention-gss.html.

8. Elizabeth Drescher, *Choosing Our Religion: The Spiritual Lives of America's Nones* (Oxford: Oxford University Press, 2016).

9. Catherine Cornille, ed., *Many Mansions? Multiple Religious Belonging and Christian Identity* (Maryknoll, NY: Orbis, 2002); Joseph Cheah, "Spiritual but Not Religious, Multiple Religious Practice, and Traditional Catholic Identities," in *World Christianity: Perspectives and Insights*, ed. Jonathan Y. Tan and Anh Q. Tran, SJ (Maryknoll, NY: Orbis, 2016), 300–317; Joseph Prabhakar Dayam and Peniel Rajkumar, eds., *Many Yet One? Multiple Religious Belonging* (Geneva: World Council of Churches, 2016).

10. Harley Talman and John Jay Travis, eds., *Understanding Insider Movements: Disciples of Jesus within Diverse Religious Communities* (Pasadena, CA: William Carey, 2016); William A. Dyrness, *Insider Jesus: Theological Reflections on New Christian Movements* (Downers Grove, IL: IVP Academic, 2016).

11. See Robert C. Fuller, *Spiritual, but Not Religious: Understanding Unchurched America* (Oxford: Oxford University Press, 2001); Ryan K. Bolger,

ed., *The Gospel after Christendom: New Voices, New Cultures, New Expressions* (Grand Rapids: Baker Academic, 2012).

12. My own typology differs from but in some ways maps onto the third through fifth points of Christian Smith and Patricia Snell's sixfold categorization: committed traditionalists, selective adherents, spiritually open, religiously indifferent, religiously disconnected, and irreligious. See Smith and Snell, *Souls in Transition*, chap. 7. Only in hindsight will clarity emerge, but while we are in the midst of this emerging revolution, we need to comprehend some of the broad strokes in order to attend to our own concerns regarding theological education.

13. Nancy Tatum Ammerman, *Sacred Stories, Spiritual Tribes: Finding Religion in Everyday Life* (Oxford: Oxford University Press, 2013), chap. 6; Lillian Daniel, *When "Spiritual but Not Religious" Is Not Enough: Seeing God in Surprising Places, Even the Church* (New York: Jericho, 2013); Linda A. Mercadante, *Belief without Borders: Inside the Minds of the Spiritual but Not Religious* (Oxford: Oxford University Press, 2014).

14. T. Scott Gross, *Millennial Rules: How to Connect with the First Digitally Savvy Generation of Consumers and Employees* (New York: Allworth, 2014); cf. Michel Serres, *Thumbelina: The Culture and Technology of Millennials*, trans. Daniel W. Smith (London: Rowman & Littlefield, 2015).

15. Jason Dorsey, "iGen Tech Disruption: 2016 National Study on Technology and the Generation *after* Millennials," Center for Generational Kinetics, 2016, https://genhq.com/wp-content/uploads/2016/01/iGen-Gen-Z-Tech-Disruption-Research-White-Paper-c-2016-Center-for-Generational-Kinetics.pdf.

16. See Yomi Kazeem, "Africa Is the Youngest Continent in the World," *Quartz*, 2017, https://www.theatlas.com/charts/HklQpE-4-.

17. Wanjiru M. Gitau, *Megachurch Christianity Reconsidered: Millennials and Social Change in African Perspective* (Downers Grove, IL: IVP Academic, 2018), 48.

18. Heidi A. Campbell and Stephen Garner, *Networked Theology: Negotiating Faith in Digital Culture* (Grand Rapids: Baker Academic, 2016), chap. 2.

19. Kioh Shim, "John Wesley's Eucharist and the Online Eucharist" (PhD diss., University of Birmingham, UK, 2013), http://etheses.bham.ac.uk/4398/1/Shim13PhD.pdf.

20. Craig von Buseck, *NetCasters: Using the Internet to Make Fishers of Men* (Nashville: B&H, 2010).

21. See also White, *Rise of the Nones*, chaps. 3–4.

22. See Pauline Hope Cheong et al., eds., *Digital Religion, Social Media, and Culture: Perspectives, Practices, and Futures* (New York: Lang, 2012).

23. E.g., Curtis J. Bonk, *The World Is Open: How Web Technology Is Revolutionizing Education* (San Francisco: Jossey-Bass, 2009).

24. I am reviewing the first page proofs of this book during the spring of 2020, almost two months into the shelter-in-place quarantine effected by the coronavirus global pandemic. The issues discussed in this section of the book about the electronic church, relatively unknown two months ago, have now been experienced by people all over the world. If our participation in the church is being gradually transformed from week to week, higher education after COVID-19 will probably never be the same. The trends overviewed in this chapter may become the norm for theological education more quickly than we had anticipated.

25. See Amos Yong, "Liberating and Diversifying Theological Education: A Subversive or Empowering Aspiration?," *CrossCurrents* 69, no. 1 (2019): 10–17.

26. Stephen D. Lowe and Mary E. Lowe, "Spiritual Formation in Theological Distance Education: An Ecosystems Model," *Christian Education Journal* 7, no. 1 (2010): 85–102; Benjamin K. Forrest and Mark A. Lamport, "Modeling Spiritual Formation from a Distance: Paul's Formation Transactions with Roman Christians," *Christian Education Journal* 10, no. 1 (2013): 110–24.

27. See Amos Yong, "Incarnation, Pentecost, and Virtual Spiritual Formation: Renewing Theological Education in Global Context," in *A Theology of the Spirit in Doctrine and Demonstration: Essays in Honor of Wonsuk and Julie Ma*, ed. Teresa Chai (Baguio City, the Philippines: Asia Pacific Theological Seminary Press, 2014), 27–38.

Chapter 4

1. See also William R. Herzog III, *Jesus, Justice, and the Reign of God: A Ministry of Liberation* (Louisville: Westminster John Knox, 1999).

2. Those who recall David Tracy's argument from almost a generation ago regarding the three publics of theological endeavor as the societal, the academic, and the ecclesial might intuit that the three parts of this volume traverse these domains, starting with the church, moving now to the societal (what I am calling the public sphere), and then attending later to academia and its various tasks. We are merely observing this "correlation" rather than using it as a structural principle for organizing this text. See David Tracy, *The Analogical Imagination: Christian Theology and the Culture of Pluralism* (New York: Crossroad, 1981), chap. 1.

3. E.g., Robert K. Greenleaf, *Seminary as Servant: Essays on Trusteeship*, rev. ed. (Peterborough, NH: Windy Row, 1983), 27–44; Max L. Stackhouse, *Ap-*

ologia: Contextualization, Globalization, and Mission in Theological Education (Grand Rapids: Eerdmans, 1988); Robert Banks, *Reenvisioning Theological Education: Exploring a Missional Alternative to Current Models* (Grand Rapids: Eerdmans, 1999); Bernhard Ott, *Beyond Fragmentation: Integrating Mission and Theological Education* (Carlisle, UK: Regnum, 2001); Peter F. Penner, ed., *Theological Education as Mission* (Erlangen, Germany: Neufeld Verlag Schwarzenfeld; Prague: International Theological Seminary of the European Baptist Federation, 2005).

4. See James F. Engel and William A. Dyrness, *Changing the Mind of Missions: Where Have We Gone Wrong?* (Downers Grove, IL: InterVarsity, 2000), 67–74, 86–88.

5. E.g., Michael W. Stroope, *Transcending Mission: Eclipse of a Modern Tradition* (Downers Grove, IL: IVP Academic, 2017).

6. See Angel Daniel Santiago-Vendrell, *Contextual Theology and Revolutionary Transformation in Latin America: The Missiology of M. Richard Shaull* (Eugene, OR: Pickwick, 2010).

7. Craig L. Nissan, *The Vitality of Liberation Theology*, Missional Church, Public Theology, World Christianity 3 (Eugene, OR: Pickwick, 2012).

8. Miguel Alvarez, *Integral Mission: A New Paradigm for Latin American Pentecostals* (Oxford: Regnum, 2016); cf. Graham Hill, *Global Church: Reshaping Our Conversations, Renewing Our Mission, Revitalizing Our Churches* (Downers Grove, IL: IVP Academic, 2016).

9. David J. Bosch, *Transforming Mission: Paradigm Shifts in Theology of Mission*, twentieth anniversary ed. (Maryknoll, NY: Orbis, 2011), chap. 12.

10. Bosch, *Transforming Mission*, 510–20.

11. Daniel White Hodge, *Homeland Insecurity: A Hip-Hop Missiology for the Post–Civil Rights Context* (Downers Grove, IL: IVP Academic, 2018).

12. Kristen Welch and Abraham Ruelas, *The Role of Female Seminaries on the Road to Social Justice for Women* (Eugene, OR: Wipf & Stock, 2015), 92.

13. E.g., Paul S. Chung, *Public Theology in an Age of World Christianity: God's Mission as Word-Event* (New York: Palgrave Macmillan, 2010).

14. See Miroslav Volf, *A Public Faith: How Followers of Christ Should Serve the Common Good* (Grand Rapids: Brazos, 2011).

15. Colleen Mary Mallon's book in this series emerges from navigating this tension vis-à-vis lay Roman Catholic education that engages the world of public health care.

16. See Amos Yong, *In the Days of Caesar: Pentecostalism and Political Theology* (Grand Rapids: Eerdmans, 2010), chap. 3.

17. See Amos Yong, *Who Is the Holy Spirit? A Walk with the Apostles* (Brewster, MA: Paraclete, 2011).

18. James Emery White, *The Rise of the Nones: Understanding and Reaching the Religiously Unaffiliated* (Grand Rapids: Baker Books, 2014), 49.

19. Steven Bouma-Prediger, *For the Beauty of the Earth: A Christian Vision for Creation Care*, 2nd ed. (Grand Rapids: Baker Academic, 2010).

20. See Barbara Brown Zikmund and Amos Yong, eds., *Remembering Jamestown: Hard Questions about Christian Mission* (Eugene, OR: Pickwick, 2010).

21. See Yong, *Mission after Pentecost: The Witness of the Spirit from Genesis to Revelation*, Mission in Global Community (Grand Rapids: Baker Academic, 2019), chap. 4, section 4.1.

22. Michael J. Gorman, *Reading Revelation Responsibly: Uncivil Worship and Witness—Following the Lamb into the New Creation* (Eugene, OR: Cascade, 2011).

23. E.g., Colin Bell and Robert S. White, eds., *Creation Care and the Gospel: Reconsidering the Mission of the Church* (Peabody, MA: Hendrickson, 2016); John Mark Hicks, Bobby Valentine, and Mark Wilson, *Embracing Creation: God's Forgotten Mission* (Abilene, TX: Abilene Christian University Press, 2016).

24. See Frank D. Macchia, *Justified in the Spirit: Creation, Redemption, and the Triune God* (Grand Rapids: Eerdmans, 2010).

25. See James K. A. Smith, *You Are What You Love: The Spiritual Power of Habit* (Grand Rapids: Brazos, 2016).

26. See Amos Yong, *Hospitality and the Other: Pentecost, Christian Practices, and the Neighbor* (Maryknoll, NY: Orbis, 2008), esp. chap. 5.

Chapter 5

1. See Scott Carlson, *Sustaining the College Business Model: How to Shore Up Institutions Now and Reinvent Them for the Future* (Washington, DC: Chronicle of Higher Education, 2018), 17.

2. See Maria Nedeva, "New Tricks and Old Dogs? The 'Third Mission' and the Re-production of the University," in *World Yearbook of Education 2008—Geographies of Knowledge*, ed. Debbie Epstein (London: Routledge, 2007), 85–103, and Emmanuel O. Bellon, *Leading Financial Sustainability in Theological Institutions: The African Perspective* (Eugene, OR: Pickwick, 2017), chap. 7.

3. See also Larry A. Smith, Marcos Orison de Almeida, and Desta Heliso, "On the Economics of Theological Education," *Insights Journal* 1, no. 1 (2015): 30–43.

4. See J. Nelson Kraybill, *Imperial Cult and Commerce in John's Apocalypse*,

Journal for the Study of the New Testament Supplement 132 (Sheffield: Sheffield Academic Press, 1996); also Yong, *Revelation*, Belief: A Theological Commentary on the Bible (Louisville: Westminster John Knox, 2021), chap. 30.

5. See Neil Selwyn, *Digital Technology and the Contemporary University: Degrees of Digitization* (London: Routledge, 2014).

6. Long ago articulated by Greville Rumble, *The Costs and Economics of Open and Distance Learning* (London: Routledge, 1997).

7. Cf. C. Neal Johnson, *Business as Mission: A Comprehensive Guide to Theory and Practice* (Downers Grove, IL: IVP Academic, 2010).

8. E.g., W. Jay Moon and Fredrick J. Long, *Entrepreneurial Church Planting: Engaging Business and Mission for Marketplace Transformation* (Wilmore, KY: GlossaHouse, 2018).

9. Kathryn Tanner, *Christianity and the New Spirit of Capitalism* (New Haven: Yale University Press, 2019), argues that if the neoliberal economy has disciplined all of us individually into the supply-and-demand commitments of a zero-sum competitive market, Christian faith and its practices of communal solidarity can free us from the chains of such a rivalrous mentality of subservience; the analysis that follows provides a parallel argument vis-à-vis the work of theological education.

10. See Amos Yong, *In the Days of Caesar: Pentecostalism and Political Theology* (Grand Rapids: Eerdmans, 2010), chap. 7.

Chapter 6

1. Michael Battle, "Teaching and Learning as Ceaseless Prayer," in *The Scope of Our Art: The Vocation of the Theological Teacher*, ed. L. Gregory Jones and Stephanie Paulsell (Grand Rapids: Eerdmans, 2002), 155–70; James E. Loder Jr., *Educational Ministry in the Logic of the Spirit*, ed. Dana R. Wright (Eugene, OR: Cascade, 2018), chap. 11.

2. See Amos Yong, *The Hermeneutical Spirit: Theological Interpretation and the Scriptural Imagination for the 21st Century* (Eugene, OR: Cascade, 2017), chap. 2.

3. Cf. James K. A. Smith, *Desiring the Kingdom: Worship, Worldview, and Cultural Formation* (Grand Rapids: Baker Academic, 2009); Diane J. Chandler, *Christian Spiritual Formation: An Integrated Approach for Personal and Relational Wholeness* (Downers Grove, IL: IVP Academic, 2014).

4. Willie James Jennings's book in this series provides a much richer account of embodied intimacy vis-à-vis the tasks and challenges of theological

learning; see also Dale M. Coulter and Amos Yong, eds., *The Spirit, the Affections, and the Christian Tradition* (Notre Dame: University of Notre Dame Press, 2016).

5. See Love L. Sechrest, *A Former Jew: Paul and the Dialectics of Race*, Library of New Testament Studies 410 (New York: T&T Clark, 2010).

6. See Daniel I. Aleshire, "Gifts Differing: The Educational Value of Race and Ethnicity," *Theological Education* 45, no. 1 (2009): 1–18; for an update of the development and expansion of Aleshire's vision for theological education, see his book in this series.

7. Also Yong, *The Missiological Spirit: Christian Mission Theology for the Third Millennium Global Context* (Eugene, OR: Cascade, 2014).

8. Carnegie Samuel Calian, *The Ideal Seminary: Pursuing Excellence in Theological Education* (Louisville: Westminster John Knox, 2002), chap. 7.

9. Cf. Yong, *Mission after Pentecost: The Witness of the Spirit from Genesis to Revelation*, Mission in Global Community (Grand Rapids: Baker Academic, 2019), chap. 6, section 6.10.

10. See Willie James Jennings, *The Christian Imagination: Theology and the Origins of Race* (New Haven: Yale University Press, 2011), and Oscar García-Johnson, *Spirit outside the Gate: Decolonial Pneumatologies of the American Global South* (Downers Grove, IL: IVP Academic, 2019); cf. Timothy Reagan, *Non-Western Educational Traditions: Local Approaches to Thought and Practice,* 4th ed. (New York: Routledge, 2018).

11. David S. Cunningham, "Hearing and Being Heard: Rethinking Vocation in the Multi-faith Academy," in *Hearing Vocation Differently: Meaning, Purpose, and Identity in the Multi-faith Academy*, ed. David S. Cunningham (Oxford: Oxford University Press, 2019), 7, 14.

Chapter 7

1. Lesslie Newbigin, *The Gospel in a Pluralist Society* (Grand Rapids: Eerdmans, 1994), chap. 18.

2. E.g., Shawn B. Redford, *Missiological Hermeneutics: Biblical Interpretation for the Global Church* (Eugene, OR: Wipf & Stock, 2012).

3. E.g., Vince Bantu, *A Multitude of All Peoples: Engaging Ancient Christianity's Global Identity* (Downers Grove, IL: IVP Academic, 2020).

4. E.g., Jason S. Sexton and Paul Weston, eds., *The End of Theology: Shaping Theology for the Sake of Mission* (Minneapolis: Fortress, 2016).

5. Grant R. Osborne, *The Hermeneutical Spiral: A Comprehensive Introduction to Biblical Interpretation* (Downers Grove, IL: IVP, 1991); see also Bernard Lonergan, *Method in Theology* (New York: Herder & Herder, 1972).

6. See John Swinton and Harriet Mowat, *Practical Theology and Qualitative Research*, 2nd ed. (London: SCM, 2015); Claire E. Wolfteich and Annemie Dillen, eds., *Catholic Approaches in Practical Theology: International and Interdisciplinary Perspectives*, Bibliotheca Ephemeridum Theologicarum Lovaniensium 286 (Louvain: Peeters, 2016); Marvin Gilbert, Alan R. Johnson, and Paul W. Lewis, eds., *Missiological Research: Interdisciplinary Foundations, Methods, and Integration* (Pasadena, CA: William Carey, 2018).

7. E.g., J. Wentzel van Huyssteen, *The Shaping of Rationality: Toward Interdisciplinarity in Theology and Science* (Grand Rapids: Eerdmans, 1999).

8. See Amos Yong, *The Spirit of Creation: Modern Science and Divine Action in the Pentecostal-Charismatic Imagination* (Grand Rapids: Eerdmans, 2011), chap. 2.

9. See Mark J. Cartledge, *The Mediation of the Spirit: Interventions in Practical Theology* (Grand Rapids: Eerdmans, 2015).

10. Lamin Sanneh, *Translating the Message: The Missionary Impact on Culture*, rev. and expanded ed. (Maryknoll, NY: Orbis, 2010).

11. See Mark A. Noll, *Jesus Christ and the Life of the Mind* (Grand Rapids: Eerdmans, 2013).

12. We return to discuss more the interrelationship between facts and values in the Christian imagination in our final chapter. On the issue of Christian teaching and learning vis-à-vis a religiously pluralistic world, see my books, *Beyond the Impasse: Toward a Pneumatological Theology of Religions* (Grand Rapids: Baker Academic, 2003; reprint, Eugene, OR: Wipf & Stock, 2014), and *Hospitality and the Other: Pentecost, Christian Practices, and the Neighbor*, Faith Meets Faith (Maryknoll, NY: Orbis, 2008).

Chapter 8

1. Mark Jordan's book in this series focuses more on the traditional classroom but also articulates beautifully and profoundly a theological pedagogy drawn from decades of honing the craft of teaching.

2. E.g., Anton C. Vrame, *The Educating Icon: Teaching Wisdom and Holiness in the Orthodox Way* (Brookline, MA: Holy Cross Orthodox Press, 1999), 81–91; Gregory S. Clapper, *As If the Heart Mattered: A Wesleyan Spirituality* (Eugene, OR: Wipf & Stock, 2014).

3. E.g., Peter DePietro, *Transforming Education with New Media: Participatory Pedagogy, Interactive Learning, and Web 2.0* (New York: Lang, 2013); A. W. (Tony) Bates and Albert Sangrà, *Managing Technology in Higher Education:*

Strategies for Transforming Teaching and Learning (San Francisco: Jossey-Bass, 2011), chap. 2.

4. See Amos Yong, *Spirit-Word-Community: Theological Hermeneutics in Trinitarian Perspective* (Burlington, VT, and Aldershot, UK: Ashgate, 2002), part 2.

5. See Raimundo Panikkar, *The Intrareligious Dialogue* (New York: Paulist, 1978).

6. See Amos Yong, *The Dialogical Spirit: Christian Reason and Theological Method for the Third Millennium* (Eugene, OR: Cascade, 2014).

7. Consistent with the dictum of the putative father of religious studies, Max Müller (1823–1900), who famously and repeatedly quipped of the religions that the person who knows one knows none.

8. See Kim A. Case, *Intersectional Pedagogy: Complicating Identity and Social Justice* (New York: Routledge, 2016).

9. See Amos Yong, *Learning Theology: Tracking the Spirit of Christian Faith* (Louisville: Westminster John Knox, 2018), chap. 4.

10. E.g., Rebecca S. Chopp, *Saving Work: Feminist Practices of Theological Education* (Louisville: Westminster John Knox, 1995); Lucy Tatman, *Knowledge That Matters: A Feminist Theological Paradigm and Epistemology* (Cleveland, OH: Pilgrim, 2001).

11. Susan Fowler, *Multisensory Rooms and Environments: Controlled Sensory Experiences for People with Profound and Multiple Disabilities* (London: Jessica Kingsley, 2008).

12. See also Dale M. Coulter and Amos Yong, *Finding the Holy Spirit at a Christian University: Renewing Christian Higher Education* (manuscript in process), chap. 6.

13. E.g., Sondra Higgins Matthaei and Nancy R. Howell, eds., *Proleptic Pedagogy: Theological Education Anticipating the Future* (Eugene, OR: Cascade, 2014).

14. See Amos Yong, *Theology and Down Syndrome: Reimagining Disability in Late Modernity* (Waco, TX: Baylor University Press, 2007).

15. See Amos Yong, *The Bible, Disability, and the Church: A New Vision of the People of God* (Grand Rapids: Eerdmans, 2011), chap. 4.

16. Bernadette Stankard, *Our Different Gifts: A Catechist's Guide to Using Multiple Intelligences in Faith Formation* (Mystic, CT: Twenty-Third Publications, 2013).

17. See also John Swinton, "From Inclusion to Belonging: A Practical Theology of Community, Disability and Humanness," *Journal of Religion, Disability & Health* 16, no. 2 (2012): 172–90.

18. If Karl Marx famously said, "The philosophers have only *interpreted*

the world, in various ways; the point, however, is to *change* it," then long before him Jesus insisted, "You will know them by their fruits" (Matt. 7:16a); see Marx's final (eleventh) thesis in *Theses on Feuerbach*, an outline of a response to Ludwig Feuerbach (1804–1872), a fellow German philosopher who Marx felt did not go far enough politically. *Theses* was not published during Marx's lifetime but is now widely available, including on the Internet. My quotation is from the translation of *Theses* provided by Lewis S. Feuer, ed., *Marx and Engels: Basic Writings on Politics and Philosophy* (Garden City, NY: Doubleday Anchor, 1959), 245.

19. See Laura W. Perna, *Taking It to the Streets: The Role of Scholarship in Advocacy and Advocacy in Scholarship* (Baltimore: Johns Hopkins University Press, 2018).

20. See Cheryl Bridges Johns, *Pentecostal Formation: A Pedagogy among the Oppressed* (Sheffield: Sheffield Academic Press, 1993); Alexia Salvatierra and Peter Heltzel, *Faith-Rooted Organizing: Mobilizing the Church in Service to the World* (Downers Grove, IL: IVP, 2014).

21. See Marybeth Gasman, ed., *Academics Going Public: How to Write and Speak beyond Academe* (New York: Routledge, 2016).

22. See also David E. Fitch, *Faithful Presence: Seven Disciplines That Shape the Church for Mission* (Downers Grove, IL: IVP, 2016).

23. See how I read Luke and Acts in *The Hermeneutical Spirit: Theological Interpretation and the Scriptural Imagination for the 21st Century* (Eugene, OR: Cascade, 2017).

24. Peter C. Hodgson, *God's Wisdom: Toward a Theology of Education* (Louisville: Westminster John Knox, 1999); Malcolm L. Warford, ed., *Practical Wisdom on Theological Teaching and Learning* (New York: Lang, 2004).

25. See Edward Farley, *Theologia: The Fragmentation and Unity of Theological Education* (Philadelphia: Fortress, 1983), and Bonnie J. Miller-McLemore, "Practical Theology and Pedagogy: Embodying Theological Know-How," in *For Life Abundant: Practical Theology, Theological Education, and Christian Ministry*, ed. Dorothy C. Bass and Craig Dykstra (Grand Rapids: Eerdmans, 2008), 170–90.

Chapter 9

1. Or in the infinite long run, as philosopher Charles Sanders Peirce put it (or the eschatological long run, in my own retrieval of Peirce; see Yong, "The Demise of Foundationalism and the Retention of Truth: What Evan-

gelicals Can Learn from C. S. Peirce," *Christian Scholar's Review* 29, no. 3 [2000]: 563–88, at 577).

2. See Robert Cummings Neville, *Axiology of Thinking*, 3 vols. (Albany: State University of New York Press, 1981–1995).

3. See Yong, *The Kerygmatic Spirit: Apostolic Preaching in the 21st Century*, ed. Josh Samuel (Eugene, OR: Cascade, 2018).

4. See Ernest L. Boyer, *Scholarship Reconsidered: Priorities of the Professoriate* (San Francisco: Jossey-Bass, 1990), chap. 2.

5. Andrew F. Walls, "World Christianity, Theological Education and Scholarship," *Transformation* 28, no. 4 (2011): 236.

6. Michael D. Kennedy, *Globalizing Knowledge: Intellectuals, Universities, and Publics in Transformation* (Stanford, CA: Stanford University Press, 2015), 34.

7. See Richard A. Posner, *Public Intellectuals: A Study in Decline* (Cambridge, MA: Harvard University Press, 2000), part 1.

8. See Steve Fuller, *The Sociology of Intellectual Life* (Los Angeles: SAGE, 2009), chap. 4.

9. If Amitai Etzioni, introduction to *Public Intellectuals: An Endangered Species?*, ed. Amitai Etzioni and Alyssa Bowditch (Lanham, MD: Rowman & Littlefield, 2006), calls attention to the marginalization of the public intellectual in Western society at large, the situation is even more dire for theologians.

10. See my essay "The Spirit, the Common Good, and the Public Sphere: The 21st Century Public Intellectual in Apostolic Perspective," in *Public Intellectuals and the Common Good*, ed. Todd Ream, Jerry Pattengale, and Chris Devers (Downers Grove, IL: IVP Academic, 2021).

11. See Martin Weller, *The Digital Scholar: How Technology Is Transforming Scholarly Practice* (London: Bloomsbury Academic, 2011), and Paul Horwitz, "Of Mirrors and Media: The Blogger as Public Intellectual," in *Public Intellectuals in the Global Arena: Professors or Pundits?*, ed. Michael C. Desch (Notre Dame: University of Notre Dame Press, 2016), 214–46.

12. See John Willinsky, *The Access Principle: The Case for Open Access to Research and Scholarship* (Cambridge, MA: MIT Press, 2006).

13. Ada María Isasi-Díaz, Mary McClintock Fulkerson, and Rosemary P. Carbine, eds., *Theological Perspectives for Life, Liberty, and the Pursuit of Happiness: Public Intellectuals for the Twenty-First Century* (New York: Palgrave Macmillan, 2013), xiv.